# Developing Reflective Practice
# in the Early Years

# Developing Reflective Practice in the Early Years

Edited by

*Alice Paige-Smith and Anna Craft*

 Open University Press

Open University Press
McGraw-Hill Education
McGraw-Hill House
Shoppenhangers Road
Maidenhead
Berkshire
England
SL6 2QL

email: enquiries@openup.co.uk
world wide web: www.openup.co.uk

and Two Penn Plaza, New York, NY 10121-2289, USA

First published 2008

A catalogue record of this book is available from the British Library

ISBN:   9780335222773 (pb)    9780335222780 (hb)
ISBN:   0335222773 (pb)       0335222781 (hb)

Library of Congress Cataloguing-in-Publication Data
CIP data applied for

Typeset by BookEns Ltd, Royston, Herts.
Printed and bound in the UK by Bell and Bain Ltd, Glasgow

The McGraw·Hill Companies

# Contents

# List of Figures

# Notes on the contributors

**Naima Browne** is a freelance early years consultant. She taught for several years in nurseries and schools in London and worked as the early years advisory teacher for bilingualism and equal opportunities. For 15 years she was a university lecturer involved in the initial training of early years and primary teachers, developing and teaching on early years professional development courses, early years MA courses and supervising PhD students. As an early years consultant she provides support and training for early years professionals working in a range of settings, speaking and running workshops at various early years conferences. Most recently she has supported practitioners in Southwark who have been developing their transition practices into and out of children's centres. She has also produced a training pack to help practitioners reflect on various aspects of transition. Naima is an active researcher in the field of early years and her work has been published in a range of books and professional and academic journals. Her books include *Young Children's Literacy Development* (Open University Press, 1990) and *Gender Equity in the Early Years* (Open University Press, 2004).

**Anna Craft**, once a primary school teacher, is Professor of Education at the University of Exeter and the Open University. She has also worked at London Metropolitan University, in curriculum development for the National Curriculum Council and for four years held a Visiting position at Harvard University. She currently teaches at foundation degree, undergraduate, master's and doctoral level, with a particular focus on creativity and future learning, especially in early years and primary education. She is founding co-editor of the journal *Thinking Skills and Creativity* and a founding convenor of the British Educational Research Association Special Interest Group, Creativity in Education. She directs several research projects focusing on creativity and education futures, with a particular emphasis on co-participative reflective engagement of both children and adults. She has written and/or edited many books, the most recent being *Creativity in Schools: Tensions and Dilemmas* (Routledge, 2005*), Creative Learning 3–11 and How We Document it*, edited with Teresa Cremin and Pam Burnard (Trentham, 2007), and *Creativity, Wisdom and Trusteeship*, edited with Howard Gardner and Guy Claxton (Corwin Press, 2007).

**Michael Craft** is an experienced public health and health promotion professional who has worked widely with under-5s and adolescents, in the UK, in former Yugoslavia and in India, over a period of some 45 years. He has held research and teaching posts in the Universities of Greenwich (where he was joint founder of a new undergraduate Public Health degree), London and Cambridge, in regional and local NHS authorities, and has held the post of director of operations for a national charity focused on support for children under emotional pressure. He was director of a community-based health education project in Cambridge for ten years and of an NHS primary care education centre in west London. Following this project he was the training officer for an NHS unit in south London for homeless people, asylum seekers and refugees. Subsequently he was one of a team of national assessors for the National Healthy Schools programme, and was founder and principal consultant to a unique health promotion project in the municipal primary schools of Delhi. More recently he was the programme manager for the largest Sure Start programme in the London borough of Haringey, and currently is a governor in two London NHS Foundation Trust Hospitals and a member of an NHS research ethics committee.

**Caroline Jones** is a former primary school teacher. She has worked for a number of years as an educational consultant at home and abroad. She now works as consultant on developing the early years workforce at the University of Warwick. She has been involved in establishing and teaching on Early Years Foundation Degrees at the Open University and the University of Warwick. Caroline has published several chapters and the book *Supporting Inclusion in the Early Years* (Open University Press, 2004). She is currently co-authoring a book on leadership and management in early years settings (Open University Press). She has a particular interest in special educational needs and is the owner of a small group of day nurseries in the Midlands.

**Alice Paige-Smith** is a Lecturer in Education (Early Years) at the Open University, Department of Education. In this role she is chair of courses within the Foundation Degree in Early Years and is a tutor on the Doctorate in Education. She has worked as an early years teacher in a number of settings, including special and mainstream schools. Her research interests are in the areas of inclusive education, professional development and early years practitioners, early intervention and parental involvement. She has carried out action research and has published a range of texts related to her research interests.

**Linda Pound** has worked in three universities and was an LEA inspector responsible for the early years for almost ten years. In addition she has been head of a nursery school and deputy head of a primary school. In her current role as an education consultant she provides training for early years practitioners around the country and overseas. She is currently an assessor for the National Professional Qualification in Integrated Centre Leadership (NPQICL). Linda writes extensively for a range of audiences – her most recent book is a second edition of *Supporting Mathematical Development in the Early Years* (Open University Press, 2006). Her major areas of interest are learning and curriculum in the early years. She is involved in advice and support throughout the early years sector in the UK and overseas.

**Michael Reed** qualified as a teacher and held senior positions in schools and thereafter as a university lecturer. His career has involved developing and managing a large day nursery, and running this successfully for over 17 years. He also developed a company involved in educational consultancy and an independent training centre for vocational qualifications in early years care and education. He has worked on projects for the Open University, forming part of the course development and writing team for the Early Years Foundation Degree. He has been a tutor for that programme and written a number of publications. Most recently, he has taught at the University of Worcester on the National Professional Qualification in Integrated Centre Leadership (NPQICL) and the Foundation Degree in Early Years. He lives in Herefordshire.

**Jonathan Rix** is lecturer in Inclusion, Curriculum and Learning at the Open University, writing and chairing courses on inclusion and early years. He has worked in education in many different settings. He spent 13 years as a support teacher in a Hackney secondary school, as well as working in theatre-in-education, as a writer-in-residence in prisons, and with community arts groups in different parts of the UK. He has won awards as a novelist, playwright and author of audio tour guides, as well as being a contributor to two books on theatre history, and the academic adviser on two Open University/BBC series: *School Day* and *Nobody's Normal*. Jonathan spent five years on the committee of Tiggers Playgroup, Balcombe, and is a member of the National Portage Association Executive. He has researched parental perspectives on early intervention, and worked as an adviser for the Departments for Education and Skills and Department of Health Early Support Programme. Jonathan has also researched inclusive pedagogies, including the simplification of language, as well as examining issues of access to heritage sites for people with learning difficulties. He is a trustee of the Rix Centre at the University of East London.

**Elizabeth Wood** is Professor of Early Childhood Education at the University of Exeter. She taught in infant and nursery classes for eight years, and was head of a nursery department in a primary school. She leads the Early Years

PGCE and MEd programmes, teaches on a range of master's and doctoral programmes, and is involved with school-based research and CPD partnerships in south-west England and Wales. Her research interests include: the role of play in lifelong learning; teachers' professional knowledge and practice; curriculum, pedagogy and assessment in early childhood education; and policy issues. She has published widely in these areas, both nationally and internationally, including the following books: *The Routledge Falmer Reader in Early Childhood Education* (Routledge Falmer, 2008); with J. Attfield *Play, Learning and the Early Childhood Curriculum* (Paul Chapman Press, 2005), and with N. Bennett and S. Rogers *Teaching Through Play: Teachers' Thinking and Classroom Practice* (Open University Press, 1997).

Background image on front cover supplied by Ruth Churchill Dower of Isaacs UK. More details at www.isaacs.uk.co.uk and www.earlyarts.co.uk.

# Foreword

*Peter Moss*

As early childhood education and care rises up the policy agenda, with increased investment and expanding services, important choices face us in connection with these services. One set of choices concerns our images or understandings – of children, of early childhood institutions and of the workers in these institutions. Our choices here are important, because they are productive of policy, provision and practice. If, for example, we choose an image of the early childhood institution as a place for applying technologies to children to deliver predetermined and normative outcomes, let us say for the sake of argument developmental or early learning goals, then the worker will be understood as a technician, tasked to follow prescribed procedures to ensure the technologies are performed effectively and the required outcomes delivered exactly.

But we – as communities of practitioners, as local communities, as societies – can choose, through democratic political process, to adopt other images or understandings of the early childhood institution. For example, we could choose to see it as a public space or forum, a place of encounter 'in which children and adults participate together in projects of social, cultural, political and economic significance' (Dahlberg *et al.* 2007: 73). Some of the outcomes of these projects may be predetermined, but others need not be. So, the early childhood institution is understood not only as a meeting place or forum, but also as a laboratory or workshop, capable of creating the unexpected, the new, the amazing, and of challenging our preconceptions, our norms and our categorizations, all of which govern us and constrict what we expect of ourselves and others.

Aldo Fortunati, drawing on many years of pedagogical work in a Tuscan commune, gives a vivid description of the worker needed for this image of the nursery:

> [The early childhood worker needs to be] more attentive to creating possibilities than pursuing predefined goals ... [to be] removed from the fallacy of certainties, [assuming instead] responsibility to choose, experiment, discuss, reflect and change, focusing on the organisation of opportunities rather than the anxiety of pursuing outcomes, and maintaining in her work the pleasure of amazement and wonder. (Fortunati 2006: 37)

In many respects, the worker that Fortunati envisages could be described as the subject of this book: the reflective professional practitioner, in marked contrast to the worker-as-technician. In its exploration of reflective practice and the reflective practitioner, this book makes an important contribution to the debate needed about the future direction of early childhood education and care.

From my perspective, and influenced very much by the pedagogical theories and practices from Reggio Emilia – a local experience of global importance referred to by several contributors to this book[1] – the concept of reflective practice is about a rigorous process of meaning-making, a continuous process of constructing theories about the world, testing them through dialogue and listening, then reconstructing those theories – what in Reggio they term a 'pedagogy of listening', applicable to children and adults alike. It is a necessarily subjective process since, as Carlina Rinaldi comments, 'there is no objective point of view that can make observation neutral' – though, as Carlina also reminds us, this is a strength, not a limitation: 'We are sometimes frightened by subjectivity because it means assuming responsibility. So our search for objectivity is often driven by the fear of taking on responsibility' (Rinaldi 2005: 128).

Reflection, too, is a dialogic process. Sometimes that dialogue may be with the self, taking place apart from others – what Rinaldi refers to as 'interior listening, listening to ourselves' (Rinaldi 2005: 65). But much of the time reflection involves relationships with others, listening to others and being listened to. It is, as this book makes clear, something to be practised collectively, as part of, but also contributing to, a 'community of practice'. Rinaldi also reminds us that dialogue can and should be more than just an exchange of views: it has 'a capacity for transformation ... where you lose absolutely the possibility of controlling the final result' (2005: 184). A theme, therefore, emerging is the potential of reflective practice to loosen the constraints of predictable outcomes and received wisdom; to expose the practitioner to new perspectives, new possibilities, new understandings; to open her up to being surprised, amazed and even lost.

For reflective practice to flourish, we need to give thought to the conditions that will support such flourishing. As contributors to this book note, time and space are essential, but often lacking – for why would technicians need such luxuries? Necessary, too, is a well-educated workforce, whose education equips them with an understanding of the importance, the theory and the process of reflection. I am writing this Foreword in New Zealand, whose ten-year strategic plan for early childhood education has set an ambitious goal for the early years workforce in centre-based services: that by 2012 all should have a graduate-level 'early years teacher' qualification (or

---

[1] To read more about Reggio Emilia, see Giudici, Krechevsky and Rinaldi (2001), Rinaldi (2006) and Dahlberg, Moss and Pence (2007).

be in training for this qualification) (New Zealand Ministry of Education 2002). This makes the English goal of one graduate 'early years professional' per nursery by 2015 seem timid and inadequate, and hardly conducive to the kind of reflective practice envisaged in this book.

This well-educated professional needs certain qualities. In addition to being comfortable with subjectivity and dialogue, she or he needs to be able to accept, indeed value, uncertainty or, in Fortunati's words, to be 'removed from the fallacy of certainties'. Once again Rinaldi helps us to see this as a strength, not a weakness:

> [Uncertainty is a] quality that you can offer, not only a limitation. And that is very problematic in a culture in which there is punishment when you have a crisis, when you have doubts, and when you make a mistake. You have to really change your being, to recognise doubt and uncertainty, to recognise your limits as a resource, as a place of encounter, as a quality. Which means that you accept that you are unfinished, in a state of permanent change, and your identity is in the dialogue. (Rinaldi 2005: 183–184)

The reflective practitioner needs also to be curious and willing, indeed eager, to border-cross – into different disciplines, different theories and different paradigms: 'an intellectually curious person who rejects a passive approach to knowledge and prefers to construct knowledge together with others rather than simply to "consume" it' (Rinaldi 2005: 135). She, or he, needs also to be a researcher, understood as having a particular stance or attitude towards work and life, a concept picked up on in Chapter 1, by Anna Craft and Alice Paige-Smith. And she or he needs to be a critical thinker, having what Elizabeth Wood in her chapter (Chapter 7) terms a 'language of critique', able to introduce:

> a critical attitude towards those things that are given to our present experience as if they were timeless, natural, unquestionable: to stand against the current of received wisdom. It is a matter of introducing a kind of awkwardness into the fabric of one's experience, of interrupting the fluency of the narratives that encode that experience and making them stutter. (Rose 1999: 20)

In short, the reflective practitioner needs to be aware of the multiplicity of perspectives that are available for thinking about any practice, and to be able to apply these to think differently and (as Jonathan Rix puts it in Chapter 5) to reframe problems. The other side of the coin is to have the capacity and desire to question dominant discourses, those 'regimes of truth' that seek to determine what we can and cannot think and do, 'interrupting their fluency ... and making them stutter'.

Other conditions conducive to reflective practice are relationships that support dialogue, rigorous subjectivity and critical thinking: with other practitioners, with children and parents sharing the everyday life and work of the nursery, but also with what might be termed 'critical friends', like the *pedagogistas* in Reggio Emilia (and elsewhere in northern Italy), experienced and well-qualified professionals each of whom works closely with practitioners in a small group of nurseries to deepen reflection on practice. Tools, too, are necessary, most obviously pedagogical documentation, referred to in several chapters of this book, a process of making practice and learning visible, and subject to interpretation, critical analysis and dialogue. Now found in many parts of the world, pedagogical documentation has its origins in Italy with innovative pedagogical thinkers like Loris Malaguzzi, the first director of early childhood services in Reggio Emilia. His biographer notes that for him pedagogical documentation was 'an extraordinary tool for dialogue, for exchange, for sharing. For Malaguzzi it means the possibility to discuss and to dialogue "everything with everyone" ... being able to discuss real, concrete things – not just theories or words' (Hoyuelos 2004: 7).

What purposes can reflective practice serve? The answer is many, and all of them important. As a number of contributors to this book note, it is integral to continuous professional development, as necessary as good basic education. It enables deeper understanding of learning and other activities undertaken in early childhood centres (though, of course, this could be equally true of schools or any other service for children and young people), and so supports planning and improving future pedagogical work: it blurs the borders between theory, practice and research. Linked to pedagogical documentation, it has an important role to play in a participatory approach to evaluation, understanding evaluation as collective meaning making and the democratic formation of judgements of value (Dahlberg *et al.* 2007). In this and other ways, reflective practice has a major contribution to make to early childhood centres being, first and foremost, places of ethical and democratic political practice, rather than of technical practice (Dahlberg and Moss 2005), providing opportunities to discuss 'everything with everyone'.

How good it would be, too, if 'everyone' included managers, policy-makers and politicians, participating – even to a limited extent – in reflection on practice through pedagogical documentation. This might help to reverse what seems to me a troubling situation: the separation between those who work with children and families on an everyday basis and those who exercise managerial and political power, who rely for their understandings and decisions on abstract indicators, too often without the benefit of 'real, concrete things'.

Reflective practice has great potential: but it also carries risks, for as Foucault reminds us, 'everything is dangerous' – even (perhaps especially) well-meant actions undertaken by well-meaning people. A major risk is that, as Elizabeth Wood writes in this volume, 'the concept of reflective practice may be narrowly interpreted as a means of ensuring that teachers and practitioners are "delivering" the curriculum, and achieving defined learning outcomes'. The danger here is that reflective practice becomes yet another 'human technology' for governing early childhood educators, or rather for self-governing through a form of reflective practice focused on assessing one's own conformity to externally imposed norms.

For Rinaldi (2005), the possibility of getting lost through dialogue and reflection, to 'lose absolutely the possibility of controlling the final result', is a risk. But it is, she insists, also a possibility, being able to see and understand the world in a different way. All the more reason to embark on reflective practice as part of a team, as a member of a community of practice.

'Developing reflective practice in the early years' is an important ambition. But as I have argued, and as contributors to this book demonstrate, this means more than adding another technology to the repertoire of workers-as-technicians. It assumes particular understandings, qualities and values. It requires certain material conditions, ranging from education of the workforce through to ensuring time for reflective practice in everyday life. It calls for certain ethical ways of relating to the self and others: dialogic and democratic, caring and respectful, listening and being open to otherness and multiplicity. It is a long and difficult journey, with no obvious end in sight, but one that seems well worth embarking upon.

# References

Dahlberg, G. and Moss, P. (2005) *Ethics and Politics in Early Childhood Education.* London: Routledge.

Dahlberg, G., Moss, P. and Pence, A. (2007) *Beyond Quality in Early Childhood Education and Care: Languages of Evaluation* (2nd edn). London: Routledge.

Fortunati, A. (2006) *The Education of Young Children as a Community Project.* Azzano san Paulo: Edizioni Junior.

Giudici, C., Krechevsky, M. and Rinaldi, C. (eds) (2001) *Making Learning Visible: Children as Individual and Group Learners.* Cambridge, MA, and Reggio Emilia: Project Zero and Reggio Children.

Hoyuelos, A. (2004) A pedagogy of transgression, *Children in Europe*, 6 (March): 6–7.

New Zealand Ministry of Education (2002) *Pathways to the Future: A 10-Year Strategic Plan for Early Childhood Education.* Wellington: Ministry of Education.

Rinaldi, C. (2005) *In Dialogue with Reggio Emilia: Listening, Researching and Learning.* London: Routledge.

Rose, N. (1999) *Powers of Freedom: Reframing Political Thought.* Cambridge: Cambridge University Press.

# Acknowledgements

Our thanks are due to the many early years practitioners, many of them our students, whose work and studies inspired us to compile this book. We are grateful to the many settings that have welcomed us as researchers – children, parents and practitioners alike. Time spent immersed in the documentation of practice and exploration of this with those involved in it has informed much of our own thinking. Our thanks are due also to our colleagues at the Open University, the University of Exeter and beyond, whose collegial development of practice and theory about practice has nourished the book's evolution. Some of these colleagues became collaborators in the book. We are grateful, too, to Fiona Richman, our commissioning editor at Open University Press, for recognizing this book's potential.

*Alice Paige-Smith, Open University*
*Anna Craft, University of Exeter and Open University*
*May 2007*

# Introduction

Anna Craft and Alice Paige-Smith

## The rise of reflective professional practice

Reflective practice is a vital aspect of working with young children. Early years practitioners are increasingly expected to reflect on their practice in a number of ways in order to enhance their professional development. Of course there is a long tradition among early childhood practitioners, of closely observing children's learning to nurture and stimulate their learning and development. But reflective practice in early years settings in the twenty-first century looks set to become more embedded, in the sense of being a key expectation of all workers who are involved with young children's learning and development.

## Development of the early years sector

As the early years sector attracts increasing attention from policy-makers, how practitioners work with the youngest children is developing significantly from a patchwork of provision, some of it very informal, and much of it offering no career advancement for those working in it, to a much more systematic network of provision and opportunity – for children and for adults. In England, the early years of the twenty-first century have seen time and resource devoted to strategic directions for this sector, as follows.

First, early education has been given more focus, with the codifying of what children should be offered in developmental terms, from:

- birth to 3, through the publication in 2002 of *Birth to Three Matters* (David *et al.* 2002; Sure Start Unit 2002a, 2002b)
- from 3–5 (QCA/DfEE 2000), and
- in more narrowly educational terms, from 5 upwards (QCA/DfEE 1999).

Second, in 2007 the integration of provision for children aged 0–5 was unveiled in the new Foundation Stage, replacing the previous provision (QCA/DfEE 2000; Sure Start Unit 2002a, 2002b). This reflects the merging of education and care in new ways.

Third, education and care have been connected to other services such as health and welfare, and services integrated so that practitioners are now expected to work within a multi-agency context, heralded in the government's ten-year National Childcare Strategy published in December 2004, which projected the organization of early childhood care and education as coming under the umbrella of integrated children's centres.

Fourth, early childhood practice is gradually being 'professionalized', both in terms of opportunities for progression and learning, and also in terms of what is expected. The introduction in 2006 of a set of priorities for developing the early years workforce can be seen as a landmark. It reflected the government's Children's Workforce Strategy (DfES 2005a, 2006), which set out the notion of the early years professional qualified to Level 6 and proposed that there be a practitioner with Early Years Professional Status (EYPS) in every children's centre by 2010, and in every full daycare setting by 2015, and that such people would take responsibility for overseeing the introduction of the new Early Years Foundation Stage. EYPS is seen as a first step in career and professional development for practitioners. As Jane Haywood, chief executive of the Children's Workforce Development Council (CWDC), says, in the Foreword to the draft Early Years Professional National Standards, published in August 2006:

> Just as early years workers have high expectations of the children they care for, so parents and carers are entitled to have high expectations of those they entrust to look after their children. There is a great deal of high quality early years practice led by highly skilled practitioners but CWDC and its partners recognise the importance of increasing levels of training and development across the early years workforce. (CWDC 2006: 3).

Each of these elements is significant. Taken together these are remarkable changes. Education, care, health and welfare are now firmly located on the same continuum, and services that support children and their families are charged with providing joined-up thinking and support. This ambitious move reflects arguments long made by Pugh (1996), Ball (1994), Moss *et al.* (1999) and others, and supported by evidence (Scott 1989; DES 1990; Sylva *et al.* 2004) on what is most valuable in combating poverty and social exclusion in particular.

## What lies behind the changes?

Behind the changes has been a range of concerns at policy level, one being the desire to reduce child poverty, another to increase educational opportunity as part of the improvement of life chances in tackling poverty and exclusion for the most vulnerable children and their families. Another concern has been to increase affordable childcare – both pre-school and around the school day – enabling more parents of young children to work and contribute to economic growth. There has also been a recognition, as the supply of childcare has expanded, that provision varies in quality, and so there has been a concern to standardize this, to articulate what is seen to be of high quality, and to provide much better education and career continuity for those working with children aged 0–8.

## Where does reflective practice come in?

Moss and Petrie (2002) urge us to consider how we work with children, to be more focused on how we construct the notion of childhood, how we respond to and engage with the multiple voices of children in our early childhood settings, and how we celebrate uniqueness at all levels. With the increased emphasis on new kinds of structures and professional/inter-professional relationships, they remind us that we need to be aware of what they call 'children's spaces', and caution us against thinking of our work as within 'children's services'. They remind us that in responding to and taking forward policy change, we can engage reflectively with this, so as to bring our own thoughts to it. In other words, they highlight for us that reflective practice is at the very least prompted by current change.

But more than this, the current changes expect reflection of early years practitioners. With the increasing expectation that early years practitioners should gain further qualifications comes the assumption that this will involve engaging with a body of knowledge about their practice. This involves a level of theoretical understanding about children's learning and participation in early years settings, and being able to reflect on how the literature, policy and theory relate to practice. Whereas this has traditionally formed an aspect of early years teachers' practice, it is now expected increasingly of the early years practitioner, and in particular of those attaining the graduate equivalent Early Years Professional Status (DfES 2006). This has already, as Potter and Richardson (1999) and Collins and Simco (2006) note, proved to be a challenging agenda in primary schools, where vastly increased numbers of teaching assistants are expected to know 'how to reflect and improve' (DfES 2005b: 12) and yet evidence suggests few efforts focused on supporting the development of such skills (Lee 2002).

This book explores some of the ways in which early years practitioners can engage with practice and relate to relevant policy and literature in the early years. It is written in particular for early years practitioners working in early years settings for children aged 0–8 years, such as children's centres, nurseries and schools, that have expectations on them to fulfil external requirements and standards from national policy on their curriculum and pedagogy provided for the children.

Understanding the national policy changes required to be implemented by early years providers is a key aspect of this book. We intend that the book will enable early years professionals, in a variety of settings, including children's centres, day nurseries, playgroups and, in the case of childminders, the home setting, to engage with both local and national policy expectations for the requirements on curriculum provision and children's experiences.

The authors within the book explore a range of issues and approaches to fostering reflective practice in early childhood settings. They take a pragmatic approach – in exploring what is expected of early years practitioners and offering practical strategies in many cases, but several also take a critical slant, problematizing the changes in provision and in the workforce, and asking what issues may arise from the development of policy in the ways undertaken so far.

The book is divided into three parts, the first focused on what being a reflective early years practitioner means (thinking about this from a general perspective, then in terms of professional development and leadership). The second part asks how reflective practice informs work with children (in four key areas), and the third part explores the leading edge of reflective practice: different aspects of working in a community of practice.

In the three chapters that constitute Part 1, we explore from different perspectives what being a reflective practitioner involves. In Chapter 1, by Anna Craft and Alice Paige-Smith, we start by considering what we mean by reflective practice in early childhood settings, both in principle and in practice. We explore the nature of reflection on practice, discussing some commonly held distinctions such as reflection in and on action, and consider how the documentation of practice, together with the establishment of a community of practice, is integrally bound into reflecting in and on it. Documentation is explored; communities of practice are taken up later in Chapter 11. Chapter 1 draws to a close by considering some practical challenges involved in developing reflective practice in early childhood settings.

Chapter 2, by Alice Paige-Smith and Anna Craft, considers the ways in which reflective practice can be developed and supported, exploring the many roles that those associated with young children's learning may adopt, considering ways of grappling with extent or 'levels' of reflection, and expanding the notion of the reflective practitioner to include both the parent and the child. Ways of working with parents in particular are discussed and explored, as well as the policy framework and expectations around working with and reflecting alongside other professionals in practice.

Chapter 3 considers the early years professional in terms of professional development and leadership within settings and the development of the current context of early years policy. In this chapter, Linda Pound takes up the notion of leadership in early years practice, identifying multiple elements of leadership involved in caring for and educating young children. She explores the nature of 'pedagogy' and unpacks the notion of the 'pedagogue', discussing the multiple foci and relationships involved, and the need to understand leadership as both inherent in everyone's job and thus also distributed. In operationalizing how reflective leadership plays out in practice, she distinguishes between tasks, roles and responsibilities as a means by which practitioners learn to work seamlessly and reflectively. Discussing the multiple aspects and levels of accountability experienced by all early years practitioners, she suggests that through reflective practice, all practitioners have the potential to transform what they do and what children and their families experience, by recognizing their compassionate responsibilities as leaders and their capabilities to observe, to document and to reflect on these.

Part 2 considers children's learning experiences from a variety of angles. The chapters explore reflection on practice, the ways in which children's identity develops within a social context, and how practitioners may support children's idea-making. Chapter 4, by Naima Browne, explores children's social and emotional development, from a perspective that recognizes the core significance of practitioners considering identity, equity and children's rights as vital to their practice. This chapter explores the socially situated evolution of children's identities and prompts the practitioner to consider relationships between emotional well-being and identity, with an exploration of the impact of gender and culture on emotional development. Transitions are explored, and the significance of hearing what children say in supporting their emotional development briefly discussed. In the following chapter, Jonathan Rix takes the notion of situated stance further in exploring inclusion in early years settings, and the significance of practitioner attitude. He too offers a model of the child as competent, active and knowledgeable, and emphasizes the significance of hearing and recognizing children's understandings, interests, feelings and needs, while acting as part of a team to support children with special educational needs. In Chapter 6, Anna Craft explores creativity in early years settings, introducing the idea of possibility thinking at the heart of all creativity, and setting this in the context of policy for creativity in the early years in England and beyond. She distinguishes between creative practice and practice that fosters creativity, and emphasizes the role practitioners take in enabling children through valuing their creative potential while finding their way through the dilemmas involved in balancing structure and freedom in practice. She acknowledges some issues involved in the cultural saturation of creativity, and explores implications of possibility thinking for reflective practice, emphasizing the significance of documentation, ownership and pedagogical approaches that involve standing back and also engaging with others including, where appropriate, children, to make sense of documentation and reflection. In Chapter 7, Elizabeth Wood explores the ways in which observation and listening to children can be used as a tool to understand children's learning, arguing that good practitioners need to be good researchers, and that integral to reflective and critical engagement with practice, is the capacity to skilfully observe and listen to children.

Finally, Part 3 explores how the notion of a community of practice can be applied to early years professionals within a shared context of supporting children's learning and working with parents and other professionals. In Chapter 8, Caroline A. Jones discusses the extent to which the multi-agency working demanded of early years practitioners by current policy, is rhetoric or reality, illustrating ways in which effective work across universal and specialist services can improve outcomes for children, as well as discussing some of the challenges and dilemmas for practitioners, taking a practical look at what using the Common Assessment Framework as a vehicle for multi-agency working means in practice. In Chapter 9, Alice Paige-Smith, Jonathan Rix and Anna Craft argue that working with others in the early years often encompasses parents, particularly where children with learning difficulties or disabilities are concerned. The authors explore expectations of and impact on parents involved in early intervention programmes designed to support children with learning difficulties or disabilities, and their families. It suggested that such programmes, which are based on a developmental view of the child, can affect parents' and children's experiences, in that during the implementation of such programmes, the home becomes the early years setting, and parents become para-professionals in supporting their children's learning. This chapter discusses ways of understanding the nature of reflective practice that may emerge in such contexts, through the development of family-centred approaches to young children's learning. It offers a window on reflective collaboration with parents through considering a study of some parents of children with learning difficulties or disabilities, but argues that the issues are broader and could be applied to all children and their parents/families.

In Chapter 10, Michael Reed explores the place of continuing professional development within current policy and practice, setting this within a socio-political context, and then exploring practicalities for early years practitioners of designing programmes of professional development that place reflection at their heart. He explores the practicalities of generating documentation, or evidence, and the possibilities inherent in professional development for personal development planning as an early years professional.

Chapter 11, by Alice Paige-Smith and Anna Craft, explores in some detail Wenger's notion of the community of practice, and considers some ways in which this may be a useful goal and process for reflective practice in early years settings, arguing that in engaging in a community of practice, each participant takes on a leadership role in the setting. Some of the tensions inherent in the model of community of practice are discussed in relation to early years practice.

Finally, in the Postscript, Alice Paige-Smith, Anna Craft and Michael Craft explore the ways in which early years professionals may have a shared sense of identity within a policy context. The early years professional is considered to be able to develop and support reflective practice, through a model of democratic reflective practice – alongside the notion of the competent child.

# References

Ball, S. (1994) *Education Reform: A Critical and Poststructural Approach*. Buckingham: Open University Press.

Children's Workforce Development Council (CWDC) (2006) *Early Years Professional National Standards*. London: CWDC.

Collins, J. and Simco, N. (2006), Teaching assistants reflect: the way forward? *Reflective Practice*, 17(2), May: 197–214.

David, T., Goouch, K., Powell, S. and Abbott, L. (2002) *Review of the Literature to Support Birth to Three Matters: A Framework to Support Children in their Earliest Years*. London: Department for Education and Skills.

Department for Education and Skills (DfES) (2005a) http://www.everychildmatters.gov.uk/_files/4C9A11CE243627228F27EA46-CAC3F658.pdf.

Department for Education and Skills (DfES) (2005b) *Common Core of Skills and Knowledge for the Children's Workforce.* London: DfES.

Department for Education and Skills (DfES) (2006) *Children's Workforce Strategy; Building a World-Class Workforce for Children, Young People and Families.* Nottingham: DfES.

Department of Education and Science (DES) (1990) *Starting with Quality: Report of the Committee of Enquiry into the Educational Experiences Offered to Three- and Four-Year-Olds (the Rumbold Report).* London: HMSO.

Lee, B. (2002) *Teaching Assistants in Schools: The Current State of Play.* Slough: NFER.

Moss, P. and Petrie, P. (2002) *From Children's Services to Children's Spaces.* London: Routledge Falmer.

Moss, P., Petrie, P. and Poland, G. (1999) *Rethinking School: Some International Perspectives.* York: Joseph Rowntree Foundation.

Potter, C.A. and Richardson, H.L. (1999) Facilitating classroom assistants' professional reflection through video workshops, *British Journal of Special Education*, 26(1): 34–36.

Pugh, G. (ed.) (1996), *Contemporary Issues in the Early Years: Working Collaboratively for Children* (2nd edn). London: Paul Chapman Publishing, in association with the National Children's Bureau.

Qualifications and Curriculum Authority (QCA)/Department for Education and Employment (DfEE) (1999) *The National Curriculum Handbook for Primary Teachers in England.* London: QCA/DfEE.

Qualifications and Curriculum Authority (QCA)/Department for Education and Employment (DfEE) (2000) *Curriculum Guidance for the Foundation Stage.* London: QCA/DfEE.

Scott, G. (1989) *Families and Under Fives in Strathclyde.* Glasgow: Glasgow College and Strathclyde Regional Council.

Sure Start Unit (2002a) *Birth to Three Matters: A Framework to Support Children in their Earliest Years.* London: Department for Education and Skills.

Sure Start Unit (2002b) *Birth to Three Matters: An Introduction to the Framework.* London: Department for Education and Skills.

Sylva, K., Melhuish, E.C., Sammons, P., Siraj-Blatchford, I. and Taggart, B. (2004) The Effective Provision of Pre-School Education (EPPE) Project, *Technical Paper 12 – The Final Report: Effective Pre-School Education.* London: DfES/Institute of Education, University of London.

# PART 1

# What does being a reflective early years practitioner involve?

# Introduction to Part 1

## Alice Paige-Smith and Anna Craft

> Some people think she can't make it to kick the ball and run down, but she really can and she kicks the ball quite a way and then she runs down. Some people on the other team are trying to catch the ball, the really fast boys and they say: 'Oh easy, it's Sophie, we are going to catch the ball' and it goes far away and she runs and she kind of changes them.
>
> (Alexia, age 6 years)

Reflecting on how we perceive children's experiences may depend on how we view the child, and how that child participates in the early years setting. Alexia is referring to a child in her class, Sophie, who has Down syndrome. While teachers, teaching assistants and the parents were all concerned about the acceptance of Sophie into mainstream school and the provision of appropriate support, just by participating in the setting Sophie was challenging and changing attitudes. Changing perceptions and understanding more about practice related to working with young children involves the different ways and levels of reflecting on our own practice, and the experiences of the children in early years settings. During this process of reflection, our perceptions of our practice may change and develop. In this first part of the book we consider approaches to reflection on practice. In particular we explore and conceptualize reflective practice and how it can be carried out by practitioners in early years settings. There are a variety of examples from different settings, including a parent and professional reflecting on practice and carrying out action research. This part of the book also begins to conceptualize reflective practice as based on stages of analysis to enable reflection. This is linked to ways in which there can be improvements in practice. As Anna Craft and Alice Paige-Smith note in Chapter 1, by engaging in reflective practice, we effectively become researchers of our working world – in much the same way that young children are researching theirs. The ways in which we interpret our practice are also framed by our current view of practice as well as our awareness of relevant literature, or theories, case studies and research data related to a variety of early years settings. Part 1 aims to encompass a range of issues relevant to the early years practitioner, such as literacy, play, leadership and management.

# 1 What does it mean to reflect on our practice?

## Anna Craft and Alice Paige-Smith

'Forget what you are being taught at the college. This is the real world.'

These words were reported by an early childhood student to her tutor, as having been said to her by the practitioner whose setting she had been placed in. Discussed in turn by her tutor in a journal article (Callaghan 2002), the clash of culture between 'practice' and 'thinking about practice' is starkly drawn. While the context is Canadian, it is perhaps a tension experienced in common elsewhere, too.

As a newly qualified teacher practitioner working with 4 and 5 year olds in the 1980s in London, one of the authors of this chapter, Anna, certainly experienced this sort of disconnection between practice and reflecting on practice. What saved her was discovering the work of Stenhouse (1985), who described teaching as an art. He highlighted the complexities in working with young children, in developing nurturing and stimulating environments in which they might grow and learn, and the delicate balance between responsiveness and providing a clear and defined framework in which they might operate. Stenhouse also wrote persuasively about teachers-as-researchers (1980a, 1980b, 1985), embedding for many practitioners the idea of reflecting on our practice as a vital element of improving it, by carefully considering the ways children respond and then developing the curriculum appropriately.

This book is concerned with practice encompassing, but not exclusively to do with, teaching. And, as outlined in the Introduction to this book, reflection is now expected of early years practitioners in a perhaps unprecedented way.

The idea that 'practice', and 'thinking about it', are somehow completely contrasting, perhaps therefore sits uneasily with emerging practices in the early years setting, whether that is in a home-based context such as childminding or nannying might be, or an institution such as a daycare or pre-school nursery or primary school classroom, or something part way between the two, such as a voluntary toy library or a playgroup operating in a local church hall.

## Why is reflection important in early years practice?

In a recent study, researchers found that pre-school children thrive most successfully when engaging in activities that prompt deep thinking (Siraj-Blatchford *et al.* 2002). The project, Researching Effective Pedagogy in the Early Years (REPEY), noted that, in particular, environments that encouraged what the research team called 'sustained shared thinking' between adults and children, fostered the greatest linguistic, social, behavioural and cognitive progress in children. What their work demonstrated was that these kinds of engagements between adults and children rely on adults having observed sensitively what children are engaging with and how they are exploring their world, so that their conversations with children are based on these – also that the discussions develop a depth and meaning for all involved, much in the way that conversations in the home sometimes do, because the parent or carer is familiar with the context to children's remarks or engagement, as Tizard and Hughes documented in their study of nursery children's conversations at home compared to those in the nursery (Tizard and Hughes 1984). Adults who are responding in a sensitive fashion and engaging in the development of an ongoing learning experience nurture children's learning and development in a way that honours the child's own interests and perspectives, and allows space for ideas and possibilities to emerge from dialogue.

In exploring dialogue in the classroom, Wegerif (2002) suggests that successful engagement between adults and children can both provide and develop a powerful learning context, where children's thinking is developed explicitly as well as their interests. This work was taken further by Littleton *et al.* (2005), whose research demonstrated the importance of adults listening to children, and of children hearing one another too. Their work emphasizes how children develop knowledge and understanding within a social environment, and how that understanding is 'distributed' within a group.

Taking this idea into early years settings and contexts, means recognizing how important our interactions are in children's development. Reflecting on how children interact with each other, and how we interact with them, is a vital part of this. Thinking together could be seen as another way of talking about sustained shared thinking, itself integrally bound into a reflective approach to practice, as an important element of effective early years provision.

In addition to this, it has been argued that we should take note of the consequences of living and working at a time of rapid change such as we are experiencing in the early twenty-first century. So much is unknown about how conceptualizations and experiences of childhood itself are shifting, as family, social and community structures are altered very fast by developments in technology, and changes in the global and globalized economy, as well as changes in the broader physical and environmental context. Perhaps, it is suggested by Yelland and Kilderry (2005), we need in early years settings to be shifting from accepting a historical wisdom about what is right, or 'good practice', to a more inquisitive approach where, as they put it, we ask ourselves 'In what ways can we create effective learning environments?' (2005: 7). Their argument is that rapid change and uncertainty in wider society affects our decisions about all kinds of issues in our practice, including ethics, equity and culture. In other words, as practitioners we need to:

- ask ourselves about how we develop our practices so as to offer the most accessible and equitable care and education possible
- deepen our understanding of how children learn and develop at this time of rapid change, and
- develop our practices alongside other services so as to appropriately support lifelong learning and lifewide citizenship in the twenty-first century.

## What does reflective practice involve?

At around the time that Stenhouse was writing, Donald Schön (1983, 1987) was also publishing work about reflective practice. His ideas, which develop a notion of 'professional artistry' (1987: 22), provide helpful ways for us to think about reflective practice in early years settings. Schön emphasizes the complexity of the role of the professional, in contrast to earlier work by Dewey (1933) who had drawn a distinction between 'routine action' (where external circumstances, habit and tradition, and externally perceived authority, are dominant, and where reasons for practices have not been considered actively) and 'reflective action' (where actions are persistently and carefully considered and justifications developed for them). Schön's work by contrast, half a century later, emphasized that professionals continuously face unique situations that they frame in light of previous experience, and he recognized therefore the ongoing complexity, and the embedded reflection, in practice. In particular, he made a distinction between 'reflection on action' and 'reflection in action' (Schön 1987). In a nutshell, the difference between these was as follows.

*Reflection in action:* thinking on your feet.
*Reflection on action:* retrospective thinking – or thinking 'after the event'.

Schön suggested that reflection is used by practitioners when they encounter situations that are unique, and when individuals may not be able to apply known theories or techniques previously learnt. As the terms he used suggest, his idea of reflective practice was very much embedded in the action of the setting itself.

His ideas ignited the imaginations of many working with people in the public services such as health, social care and education, and have influenced practices around the world in seeking to improve these. But as Loughran (2002), working in Australia, writes, although reflective practice can offer us genuine improvement-orientated feedback on our practice, it is important that we really develop our reflection in such a way that it is shared, and such that it enables us to question assumptions that we might otherwise take for granted. As he puts it, reflection on practice should enable us to see our practice through the eyes of others.

But it is more than seeing and thinking about our practice. It is about exploring both how we feel about it as well as how we understand it. Through questioning what we do and how we might develop our practice, it builds bridges from our professional to our personal lives, and vice versa. As Williams (2002) puts it, reviewing a book (Bolton 2001) about using writing to develop reflective practice in medicine, reflective practice

> helps to establish bridges between these two areas. It helps to integrate the technical expertise of the professional with the personal and emotional qualities of the individual ... Reflective practice allows our natural instincts to interact with a professional approach. Actions are so much more powerful if they arise from both feelings and thoughts. (Williams 2002: 55)

In early years settings, where increasingly practitioners are working alongside others, there are good opportunities to share perspectives on the same activity, and to compare interpretations. This may be particularly helpful where, for example, a care professional is working alongside a health, education or welfare professional (i.e. someone bringing a different but overlapping set of sensitivities, knowledge, experience and responsibilities to the work of supporting children). The mix of cultural practices in adjacent and collaborating professional areas providing children's services means that sharing documentation of practice is both fertile and complex. We might borrow from Huberman's (1995) notion of open networks that alter practice – in his case he was focused on teaching, but it emphasizes the significance of insights that may come from outside of our own perspective and that may therefore bring new insights into our practice. These in turn may help us to develop new understanding.

By reflecting in and on our practice we are opening up the possibility, alongside others, of what Engestrom (1993) calls a 'problem space', at which we direct our engagement and a commitment to development and change. In Chapter 10 of this volume, Mike Reed explores components of reflective practice, including the explicit recognition of evidence-based reflection in the workplace, and therefore evidence gathering in the workplace, which is recognized as necessary for reflective practice but also protects confidentiality appropriately; also the recording/observation of practice through a variety of means, communication between practitioners as co-investigators, and a focus on defining and developing 'good practice'.

Pollard (2002) identified seven characteristics of reflective practice in teaching, which Warwick and Swaffield (2006) suggest are equally applicable to teaching assistants. These characteristics may also be useful to early years practitioners, some of whom are indeed teaching assistants. For Pollard, reflective practice in teaching involves:

- *active focus on goals, on how these are addressed, and the consequences of both*, alongside a concern with 'technical efficiency' (Pollard 2002: 12)
- *commitment to a continuous cycle* of monitoring practice, evaluating and revising it
- *focus on informed judgements* about practice, based on evidence
- *open-minded, responsible and inclusive attitudes*, with what Zeichner and Liston (1996) call 'an active desire to listen to more ideas than one ... and to recognise the possibility of error' (Zeichner and Liston 1996: 10)
- *capacity to re-frame own practice* in light of evidence-based reflection and also insights based on other research
- *dialogue with other colleagues*, both individuals and across groups – what MacGilchrist *et al.* (2004) suggest is integral to the 'intelligent school' – and cooperation with colleagues beyond the school – individuals, agencies, organizations
- *capacity to mediate and adapt externally developed frameworks* for practice, making reflective and appreciative judgements about when it is appropriate to innovate, and when to defend existing practices, both individually and collaboratively.

Pollard's reflective practice principles emphasize the vital mix of evidence and reflection – which implies a need to collect evidence, or to *document* practice – and the formation of a community. This latter point is explored in Chapter 11, where we discuss aspects of communities of practice.

## Documenting practice

Whether we are thinking about reflection in action (on our feet) or reflection on action (afterwards), we need to consider how we capture what it is we are reflecting on – or how we *document* it. When we document action, we could be providing an 'anchor', which helps us to access – often at a later point, if we are reflecting *on* action – all the different thoughts and feelings that we have about the event itself. Much of our documentation is held or built up informally, and consists of memories, anecdotes shared with others, children's constructions, and other artefacts such as drawings and writing. Other documentation, however, is more intentional, or formal. Commonly used means of more formalized documentation include:

- the journal (in which observations as well as reflections on these, are recorded); an idea developed further by Mike Reed in Chapter 10 of this volume
- images (digital), collected by adults and also by children, which may form a focus of reflection with children but also with other adults; documentation of children's learning can help us to create visual narratives in which their engagement and their voices are foregrounded; this is the case whether we are working with a sequence of still images or video material
- sound recordings, collected by adults and also by children, enabling us to listen to children's involvement in particular episodes
- transcriptions of what children have said in conversation with one another and with practitioners.

Sometimes documentation will be gathered in to a particular place – for example, on a special wall in the setting, or in a log for each child or a portfolio associated with the practitioner and focused around specific children.

Documenting our practice and children's learning enables us to explore with others what has engaged and focused children; it helps us to make predictions about what they know and are confident with, and what they are grappling with. It helps us to plan our work with them appropriately, for both individual and group learning (Project Zero/Reggio Children 2001). In some early years settings, and building on the practices of the Reggio Emilia pre-schools in northern Italy, practitioners share the annotations of their documentation for all involved in children's care and learning to see. The audiences may include the child, their parent(s) and/or carer(s), other staff, consultants, and others. As Carla Rinaldi, of Reggio Children, writes:

I am convinced ... that the effect of documentation (documents, notes, slides, and recordings) is not limited to making visible that which *is,* but on the contrary, by making an experience visible, documentation enables the experience to exist and thus makes it sharable and open to the 'possibles' (possible interpretations, multiple dialogues among children and adults). Therefore, I believe that narrating the learning process requires the use of verbal and visual languages not only in a narrative and analytical way, but also in a poetic, metaphorical, musical, physical, and dramatic sense.

In other words, in order to make a learning experience possible – and therefore to make it a conscious form of learning that can also be narrated – processes and language should be closely interwoven, so as to support each other reciprocally and to support the quality of the learning experience itself. What we actually have to document (and therefore bring into existence) is the 'emotionally moving' sense of the search for the meanings of life that children and adults undertake together – a poetic sense that metaphorical, analogical, and poetic language can produce and thereby express in its holistic fullness. (Rinaldi 2001: 150)

The Reggio approach places an emphasis on the arts as a means to document and make sense of learning. Perhaps the most significant element, though, about documentation, whether the Reggio approach or one's own, is that it not only makes learning visible – but it also encourages participation, in the holistic support of children's learning that takes full account of the emotional dimension. It is a focus of dialogue and interaction – it is not simply a means of 'reporting'. Thus, incorporating space in documentation for comments from parents, practitioners, children and others is a vital part of the process of undertaking it. Katz and Chard (1997) suggest that documentation adopted in this way contributes to the quality of early childhood practice in that it signals how seriously children's ideas and work are taken, and fosters awareness of practitioners in continuous planning and evaluation.

To this end, it can be useful to develop protocols for engaging with documented evidence from practice. One means of doing so is to use the Collaborative Assessment Conference (CAC), developed at Harvard University's Project Zero by Steve Seidel in collaboration with numerous early childhood educators during regular reflection sessions offered at Harvard. It comprises a means of looking more and more closely at evidence, in a pairing or small group, and provides a structure whereby judgements are formed and opinions offered, very slowly, and only after a shared 'reading' of the material has taken place. The material is seen as a 'performance of understanding' (Blythe and associates 1998; Wiske 1998). In other words, children's current understandings are seen to be manifest in their actions, which are captured in our documentation. The interpretive process focuses on the documentation itself. Drawn in part from arts practices the pair or group support one another in adhering to the following process.

## Collaborative Assessment Conference (CAC) process

### Step 1: 'Reading' the material, or performance

'I see several children at a table sharing a large piece of clay.'

### Step 2: Describing the material, or performance

'The girl in the foreground has her hands on the clay and she is making scratch marks on it; she seems to be frowning.'

### Step 3: Raising questions/speculating

'I wonder what the frown means and whether perhaps the clay is difficult to make marks on; I am wondering why the children are all sharing one lump of clay; I am wondering what the objective of this experience was; I am wondering where the girl in the foreground might want to go next in her exploration of the clay and what we could do to support this.'

### Step 4: Hearing from the presenter(s)

In other words, hearing views from the practitioner(s) responsible for collecting and selecting the material to bring to the discussion. This might include why they collected it, but also thoughts in response to questions and observations raised by others (easier to do if they have jotted down other people's thoughts during steps 1–3).

### Step 5: Discussing implications

What happens next for the children? What would be appropriate ways of developing practice next? What are the challenges and opportunities in doing so?

### Step 6: Reflecting on the protocol

How useful has the collaborative assessment conference been on this occasion? How might we adapt it for use next time? When will we use it next?

While the Project Zero CAC is just one means of formalizing reflection with others, its advantage is that it facilitates the development of an enquiring community of perspectives, it belongs to the professionals working with it, it facilitates inter-professional thinking, and it holds within it an assumption that the child is competent as a thinker and learner. It can also be adopted within the classroom or setting with children themselves.

## Challenges in reflective practice

There are numerous challenges involved in fostering reflective practice. At its most basic, making time and space to do it may be one, so that our reflection and consequent learning is not accidental. One of the authors of this chapter, Alice, found that by making space to document a specific child's learning moments in relation to literacy for the period of a morning, she noticed the significance of that child's 'mark making' during play. Through her close documentation, Alice realized that the child was linking her attempts to write her name in the office play area with her name on her coat peg in the corridor, by 'mark making' on a notepad in the play area, then running to her peg to read the letters in her name and to try sounding out the letters. She would then run back to the office play area to sound out the letters in attempting to write her name. Alice witnessed the journey back and forth, and it offered insights into how to support this child's developing literacy (Miller and Paige-Smith 2003). But the challenge is not purely in making time: it is the double act of capturing moments such as these, as well as managing children's learning experiences. The reflective practitioner simultaneously works with questions formed around children's learning experiences so as to capture them – for instance, 'How does Jacob participate in circle time?' or 'How does Priya participate during a school trip – what has she learned from the experience?' – yet simultaneously has an eye to the need to offer a framework to the children's learning.

Another challenge is how and with whom the documentation of children's learning is shared. Possibilities include one's colleagues and, of course, parents. Sharing perspectives in this way is an essential part of the development of the role of the early years professional within a variety of settings, including children's centres and schools. Such communication also encompasses children's transitions both into and onward from the setting.

Fostering reflective practice is not easy or, necessarily, straightforward. One of the very practical challenges is finding the right balance between expectations of learning through reflection and the time and experience involved in it; and the tensions that were pointed up at the start of the chapter are still live (Edwards 2000). Essentially in reflective practice we become researchers looking at our own work in order to develop and improve it. And, as Kennedy (1997) argues, discussing the relationship between research and educational practice in the United States, we need to recognize that practice and research are both situated in shifting social and political contexts. We need to be realistic about how self-study can influence our practice. Edwards talks of early years practitioners 'using practical knowledge of their professions to anticipate events and maintain control of them' (Edwards 2000: 185) and sees this as 'part of the constant cycle of interpretation and response that is at the core of informed professional action in complex settings' (2000: 185). Reflective practice, then, according to Edwards, is 'embedded in the practical knowledge of the community of practitioners ... [informing] practitioners' ways of seeing and being' (2000: 185). This is a challenging task since, as Edwards notes, it means positioning one's work and practices within the complex relationships with children, their families, other services and wider policies. And as Kennedy (1997) points out, early years practitioners are particularly affected in developing their practice by the shifts in policy occurring in the early 21st century, so some of what is changing and evolving is externally imposed.

An important challenge is how to remain open. As Huberman (1995) points out, we can nurture fresh perspectives and evolve new understandings of and approaches to our practice when we remain open to insights from others, through what he calls 'open networks'. A weakness in reflective practice, however, can come from the closed network, where ways of doing things are not open to scrutiny, re-interpretation or development. Reflective practice demands that we create opportunities to bounce our ideas off others and to co-construct understandings and ideas. In this sense having a critical friend, a mentor or a reflective practice learning set is helpful. Bringing more than one perspective to documentation of reflective practice can help to overcome subjectivity in our reflections. And, of course, in documenting and reflecting on practice, we must take due care of ethics, manifesting sensitivity to children's rights, and privacy issues so that risks are minimized.

## A reflective future?

The new graduate professional award of Early Years Professional Status (EYPS) (CWDC 2006), which has equivalent status to Qualified Teacher Status (QTS), brings with it an expansion of roles in settings for children from 0–5, and means that early years settings such as nurseries and children's centres are likely to be led by senior staff with high sensitivity to the need to understand others' perspectives. This capacity to co-construct understanding and ideas may be considered to be an essential part of the early years practitioner's role, constructing meaning alongside the children, and trying to understand children's experiences in order to support and encourage learning.

# References

Blythe, T. and associates (1998) *The Teaching for Understanding Guide*. San Francisco, CA: Jossey-Bass.

Bolton, G. (2001) *Reflective Practice: Writing and Professional Development*. Paul Chapman Publishing Ltd.

Callaghan, K. (2002) Nurturing the enthusiasm and ideals of new teachers through reflective practice, *Canadian Children* (the journal of the Canadian Association for Young Children), 27(1), Spring: 38–41.

Children's Workforce Development Council (CWDC) (2006) *Draft Early Years Professional National Standards*. http://www.cwdcouncil.co.uk/pdf/Early%20Years/Draft_EYP_Standards_Aug_2006.pdf (accessed 23 April 2007).

Dewey, J. (1933) *How we Think: A Re-statement of the Relation of Reflective Thinking in the Educative Process*. Chicago: Henry Regnery.

Edwards, A. (2000), Research and practice: is there a dialogue? in H. Penn (ed.), *Early Childhood Services: Theory, Policy and Practice*. Buckingham Philadelphia: Open University Press.

Engestrom, Y. (1993) Developmental studies of work as a testbench of activity theory: the case of primary care medical practice, in S. Chaiklin and J. Lave (eds) *Understanding Practice. Perspectives on Activity and Context*. Cambridge, UK: Cambridge University Press.

Huberman, M. (1995) Networks that alter teaching, *Teachers and Teaching: Theory and Practice*, 1(2): 193–211.

Katz, L.G. and Chard, S.C. (1997) Documentation: the Reggio Emilia approach. *Principal*, 76(5), 16–17 May.

Kennedy, M. (1997) The connection between research and practice, *Educational Researcher*, 26(7): 4–12.

Littleton, K., Mercer, N., Dawes, L., Wegerif, R., Rowe, D. and Sams, C. (2005) Talking and thinking together at Key Stage 1, *Early Years: An International Journal of Research and Development*, 25(2): 167–182.

Loughran, J.J. (2002) Effective reflective practice. In search of meaning in learning about teaching, *Journal of Teacher Education*, 53(1): 33–43.

MacGilchrist, B., Myers, K. and Reed, J. (2004) *The Intelligent School*. London: Sage.

Miller, L. and Paige-Smith, A. (2003) Literacy in four early years settings, in L. Miller and J. Devereux (eds) *Supporting Children's Learning in the Early Years*. London: Fulton.

Pollard, A. with Collins, J., Simco, N., Swaffield, S., Warin, J. and Warwick, P. (2002) *Reflective Teaching: Effective and Evidence-Informed Professional Practice*. London: Continuum.

Project Zero/Reggio Children (2001) *Making Learning Visible: Children as Individual and Group Learners*. Reggio Emilia: Reggio Children srl.

Rinaldi, C. (2001) The courage of Utopia, in C. Giudici and C. Rinaldi with Krechevsky, M. (2001) *Making Learning Visible: Children as Individual and Group Learners*. Reggio Emilia: Reggio Children.

Schön, D. (1983) *The Reflective Practitioner*. New York: Basic Books.

Schön, D. (1987) *Educating the Reflective Practitioner*. San Francisco: Jossey-Bass.

Siraj-Blatchford, I., Sylva, K., Muttock, S., Gilden, R. and Ball, D. (2002) *Researching Effective Pedagogy in the Early Years*. DfES Research Brief No. 356.

Stenhouse, L. (1980a) Curriculum research and the art of the teacher, *Curriculum*, 1: 40–44.

Stenhouse, L. (1980b) Artistry and teaching: the teacher as the focus of research and development. Paper presented at the Summer Institute on Teacher Education, Simon Fraser University, Vancouver, in D. Hopkins and M. Wideen (eds) (1984) *Alternative Perspectives on School Improvement*. Lewes: Falmer Press.

Stenhouse, L. (1985) Curriculum research, artistry and teaching, in J. Ruddock and D. Hopkins (eds) *Research as a Basis for Teaching: Readings from the Work of Lawrence Stenhouse*. London: Heinemann Educational.

Tizard, B. and Hughes, M. (1984) *Young Children Learning*. London: Fontana.

Warwick, P. and Swaffield, S. (2006) Articulating and connecting frameworks of reflective practice and leadership: perspectives from 'fast track' trainee teachers, *Reflective Practice*, 7(2), May: 247–263.

Wegerif, R. (2002) Walking or dancing? Images of thinking and learning to think in the classroom, *Journal of Interactive Learning Research*, March.

Williams, D. (2002) Book review of G. Bolton (2001) *Reflective Practice: Writing and Professional Development*. Paul Chapman Publishing Ltd, *Journal of Medical Ethics: Medical Humanities*, 28: 55–56.

Wiske, M.S. (ed.) (1998) *Teaching for Understanding: Linking Research with Practice*. San Francisco, CA: Jossey-Bass.

Yelland, N. and Kilderry, A. (2005), Against the tide: new ways in early childhood education, in N. Yelland (ed.) *Critical Issues in Early Childhood Education*. Maidenhead and New York: Open University Press/McGraw-Hill Education.

Zeichner, K. and Liston, D. (1996) *Reflective Teaching: An Introduction*. Mahwah, NJ: Lawrence Erlbaum Associates.

# 2 Developing reflective practice

## Alice Paige-Smith and Anna Craft

## Introduction

In this chapter, we explore some different ways in which reflection on practice can be developed, and draw on practice that relates to the current contexts of the early years professional who works in a variety of early years settings such as children's centres, nurseries and schools. We locate a number of different aspects of practice that can be reflected upon, developed and possibly changed and challenged, such as working with parents and other professionals and inclusive education. These are linked to approaches to children's learning and well-being as conceptualized within policy documents in England. We explore ways in which links can be made between policy, theory and practice when using methods of reflection, such as observation and diaries. Case studies of how early years practitioners can develop and change their practice are considered.

## How can reflection on practice be developed?

Sustaining effective early years practice involves reflecting on, developing and possibly changing our own practice. As suggested in Chapter 1, a shared understanding of 'reflection' among a community of practitioners, such as early years professionals, may be useful in doing so. As discussed in Chapter 1, Schön (1983) writes about how reflection *on* action, allows practitioners to spend time exploring group and individual actions. When this happens, questions and ideas are raised about activities, as well as practice. For instance, early years practitioners may change practice by focusing more on the child's perspective of their world and how they learn. In the words of a childminder who studied the Open University undergraduate Level 1 early years course *Working with Children in the Early Years*:

> I now have the ability to recognize why children do what they do and how I can use their actions to extend their learning ... I have become far more involved with what the children are doing. Where as previously I may have taken ten minutes for a cup of tea and a break while a 3 year old was absorbed with small world toys, I now observe the child in order to plan

future experiences for her, and I will also join in the play and extend the learning experience for her. The result is that she thinks we are playing together and is encouraged to play, and therefore learn, in a more educational way with me guiding and explaining as we go. (Childminder E123, Open University Course, cited in (Devereux and Paige-Smith 2004: 12)

Several years ago, one of the authors of this chapter, Alice, noticed, in her role as a parent of a child in a nursery class within a primary school in north London, the inclusion of three children with disabilities who each required one-to-one support from a learning support assistant. The allocation of support for each child was based on their requirements as set out in the statement of their special educational needs. At the same time, Alice also had another role, as a professional, being a learning support teacher in another school and also studying part-time for a master's degree. By talking with the parents of the children in the nursery class where she was volunteering, Alice understood that their child's learning support assistant's role was under threat, as the local authority was proposing to reduce the support allocated. If this were to happen, it would result in the nursery being unable to include all three of the children with special needs within its provision. Alice became involved with one family, and with the campaign that was consequently set up by parents and a voluntary organization to protect the rights of these children with statements of their special educational needs. The outcome was, in the end, positive, and the children's support was retained. However, much uncertainty was felt over the children's future in the nursery, by many associated with the school during this period – specifically the children, the parents and the support assistants.

During the period of uncertainty, as a parent Alice was able to link up with the other parents and be supportive. As a support teacher she understood that the children would be able to remain in mainstream nursery with the support assistant. Alice had drawn on her practice as a learning support teacher; she knew that their inclusion was possible, and that the assistant would be able to adapt the curriculum for the children alongside the teacher. In addition, Alice's role as a student-researcher enabled her to support the campaign to save the provision, by providing information from policy documentation about the children's legal rights to provision. Within the campaign, she became an advocate for children and their parents. Alongside the action, as a reflective practitioner and researcher she also maintained relevant documents, and wrote a reflective diary and observation notes of all the meetings attended with the parents. Alice interviewed the parents and the education officers. She subsequently gathered her reflections to write about the experience in the form of an action research case study (Paige-Smith 1996).

During the process of reflecting on the children's circumstances in the nursery, Alice's practice as a professional with relevant 'knowledge and expertise' led her to question the practice in the setting. She began to ask questions such as:

- Why was the children's inclusion under threat if they had statements of their special educational needs outlining the resources they were entitled to?
- Was this happening to other children around the country, or was it specific to that nursery and local education authority?

As a professional, Alice knew that this practice was localized within that authority, and if the children had lived three miles away in another authority their support would not have been under threat. She chose to make time to consider her actions, an important feature of reflective practice (Schön 1983). Alice also used a number of research methods to triangulate the information collected. During this process of collecting data Alice ensured that she was not making 'value judgements' about the children's education, and that she was able to place her own perspective, values and views within a wider context. While this research on practice was 'action research' as she was changing practice at the same time as carrying out the research, it relied on her reflecting not only on the actions of others, but on her own actions too.

## Levels of reflection on practice

Rosenstein (2002) notes how difficult conceptualizing reflection can be because of the many different kinds of reflection possible, noting that in a sense it is like deciding how to present oneself in terms of what clothes to wear: 'Deciding what to wear is one form of reflection, and theorizing about presentation of self (Goffman 1959) is another on the same subject at a different level' (Rosenstein 2002: 258). In the example given above, Alice found herself wearing several different 'outfits': the parent helper, the learning support teacher, the advocate and campaigner, and the researcher. She chose what to 'wear' at different times, and how to combine the different roles that each represented, to help find a resolution. In choosing what information was needed for each part of the campaigning process, she was making selections about what image to present and how to argue the case.

While Alice's story is, in some ways, an extreme example, you may be able to identify times when you select different kinds of evidence and reflection on your practice. One way of thinking about this is in terms of how deeply you are reflecting on your practice. Rosenstein (2002: 258) also suggests that examples of levels of reflection can provide a framework to help understand reflection. She draws on van Manen's (1977) four levels of reflection:

1. everyday thinking
2. incidental and limited reflection on our practical experience
3. systematic reflection with the aim of theoretical understandings and critical insights, and
4. reflection on reflection that examines how knowledge functions and how it can be applied to active understanding.

In the above examples of levels of reflection, van Manen recognizes the shift from an 'everyday' activity such as thinking to other levels that involve critical insights, perhaps relating to theoretical knowledge or deeper information about activities.

Rosenstein (2002) points to the levels constructed by Bain *et al.* (1999), which were collated through the study of the reflective journals of 35 student teachers. In this case, the levels indicate how as a practitioner we can *document* our practice as a way of being able to generalize from our experiences (Bain *et al.* 1999, in Rosenstein 2002: 259).

- *Level 1*: reporting the event as it occurred.
- *Level 2:* responding to the event in a spontaneous and emotional manner.
- *Level 3:* relating to the event in terms of past experience and knowledge.
- *Level 4:* reasoning about the event in terms of alternatives, examining assumptions, and conceptualizing characteristics of the occurrence.
- *Level 5:* reconstructing the event in terms of theories that can be applied to a broader range of experiences.

Bain's framework bears close similarities to the one proposed by van Manen, in the shift from the literal and immediate to the abstract/conceptual and theoretical. Reflection on practice can, then, facilitate our understanding. Placing what can be complex problems and issues within a context, supported by documentation, we may develop and improve practice.

Reflective practice supports ways of working with children, other professionals and, of course, parents. As partners in the reflective practice process sometimes forgotten or underestimated, let us consider working with parents.

## Working with parents

Pugh, writing about parent partnership, identifies five different kinds of roles that parents might assume in early years provision (1989: 3).

1. *As supporters:* service givers, clerical, custodial, facilitators, maintenance, fundraisers.
2. *As learners:* on parent education courses, observing their children with some explanatory help.
3. *As teachers:* taking toys/books to use at home.
4. *As classroom aides and volunteers:* preparing materials, reading stories, working with children.
5. *As policy-makers and partners:* advisory board members.

Taking the ways parents may participate a little further to look at how *involved* they are in practice, Tait (2003) points to work under way at Pen Green Centre for under-5s, in Northamptonshire (identified as a centre for excellence in early years in England). This children's centre is developing innovative ways of involving different groups of parents, through what it calls 'models of engagement':

- attendance at key concept training sessions and information exchange (parents provide information for discussion about their child's activity that has been recorded in a diary)
- home/nursery books
- home/school video
- issue-specific evenings
- family group evenings.

It measures success in terms of parents participation according to attendance. Staff at Pen Green wanted to engage fathers in particular, believing that fathers who wanted to know about their child's learning would be able to make a difference to their child's education. They found that they were more successful in engaging men when they included factual 'achievement-orientated' information on publicity materials.

Involvement is defined as: 'Sustained use of any of the models of engagement. This would include the parent who, for example, only attends groups sporadically, but who keeps his or her diary on a regular basis, and discusses the child's learning with members of the nursery staff' (Tait 2003: 52).

Encouraging parents to participate can involve a number of different approaches. Arnold (2003) describes how the practice at the Pen Green Centre involves collaborating with parents and the sharing of the pedagogy teachers use about child development theories. The approach also focuses on listening to parents' detailed information about their own children, resulting in a clearer articulation of the pedagogy used by professionals. The emphasis is on parents as 'equal and active partners' rather than 'helpers' for practitioners. This includes engagement in reflection.

## Parents as participants in reflective practice

Staff at Pen Green involved parents in setting up study groups as part of the Parents' Involvement in their Children's Learning project. This consisted of discussion groups where adults reflect on their own experiences in the past and present, as well as accessing new information regarding their child's develop-ment (Arnold 2003). The study groups involve discussions where parents compare notes with nursery staff and watch video tapes of their children playing in the nursery and at home (Arnold 2003: 62). The project places at the centre of its work with parents and children key concepts about children's development; these include children's emotional well-being and their involve-ment. Laevers' (1997) signals of well-being are used as indicators (openness and receptivity; vitality, relaxation and inner peace; enjoyment without restraints).

In the Pen Green example, parents are supported in getting to grips with the theoretical understanding and the meaning of the pedagogy used in order to support their child's learning. They are encouraged, in other words, to reflect at Level 3 of van Manen's reflection framework (1977), in that their reflection is systematically supported, with the aim of developing critical insights with practitioners. They draw on documentation (video material) of children's learning, which provides a basis for reflecting at Level 4 of Bain *et al.*'s framework (1999): reasoning about the event; examining assumptions; conceptualizing characteristics.

The practice at Pen Green and Pugh's more generalized summary of parental involvement (1989) may provide us with different ways of considering or approaching parental involvement in reflective practice. Other more detailed practices and guidance are included not only in government documents such as the *Early Years Foundation Stage* (DfES 2007) but also in documents such as the *Index for Inclusion* in the early years (Booth and Ainscow 2004). The *Index for Inclusion* provides supportive guidance for practitioners working in settings on how to change through the use of development plans by reflecting on their practice, in particular through considering values within the setting and how they relate to inclusive cultures, policies and practices. Reflective practice, in other words, is embedded in expectations held by key people in young children's lives.

# Developing practice and reflection

Chak (2006) outlines the importance of self-reflection and self-study as follows:

> engaging in self-study through systematic research on a designated issue of one's practice may be different from the making of everyday self-observations and immediate reflections on one's own practice. While an

in-depth study of a theme or an issue is the focus of a self study, when attention is selectively paid to 'noticing' this theme or issue, it is perhaps less possible in the study to capture, reflect on, and respond to a vast amount of rich dynamic interactions in everyday practice, which Schön denotes as 'reflection in action'. (Chak 2006: 56)

The distinction between *reflection in* and *reflection on* action was introduced in Chapter 1, but what Chak captures here is the significance of the everyday and the moment-by-moment observations that we make in our practice. Also significant is the personal connection that we may make to our everyday practice, which can sometimes run very deep indeed.

Kirsty Thompson, who practised as an occupational therapist in Australia, has written (2006) about how she has been unable to recall 'traumatic' experiences she had as a child when her parents were trying to access services required to support her and her family. This led to her research on how professionals work with parents, in which she reflected on her own agency, identity and experiences. Kirsty described how she came to her research question, and explains how the process of her self-reflection influenced her study of her professional practice. In the following extract Kirsty first describes the experiences of the parents in her study after the birth of their premature baby, born with a physical disability. She then links their experiences to the experiences of her own parents and how she used to hear the same story as she grew up.

> Both the parents and the child cry through alternate hours of painful therapy and tired feeding programs. They travel for appointments with the therapists and doctors not available in their area. Mother and child temporarily move away from home to be closer to the required services. The home programs and visits with professionals are often traumatic and hard work. Sometimes the parents are not sure why or how to do these therapy programs. After their initial contact with professionals in hospital they largely feel alone and a little scared that they are doing the right thing to help their child. They are told that it is up to them now if their child walks. So they do these home programs and attend these appointments hoping that their efforts will be enough.
>
> I heard this story often as I grew up. It is a story that, at least for me, ended well. My 'disability' was relatively minor and has little impact on my daily life. I am able to walk and barely recall the 'traumatic' experiences. Yet the anger and distress associated with my parents' interactions with services is still palpable in the story my parents tell today. For me, their story started a journey seeking to understand services for children with a disability and in particular, what shapes the ways that professionals work with families. What is it, for example, that influences how professionals provide instructions to parents? (Thompson 2006: 13)

The ways in which parents and professionals share information may have changed since Kirsty was a child, however 'parent partnership' and listening to parents remain key parts of documents relating to working with parents of disabled children, such as *Together from the Start* (DfES 2003b). This document identifies both effective practice and examples of how the 'rights' of parents and children should be valued by professionals (Paige-Smith and Rix 2006). Effective communication is recognized as a key principle when involving parents in early years settings and the child's education. *Together from the Start* (DfES 2003b) suggests that 'The child's name should be used at all times' and to 'remember to communicate in a way that shows respect for the child' (DfES 2003b: 13). The government report *Every Child Matters* (DfES 2003a) under-pins many early years services and identifies that there should be a stronger focus on early intervention with children identified to be 'at risk'. The sharing of information between parents, and professionals is seen as central to support children and their well-being (DfES 2003a: 21) (Figure 2.1).

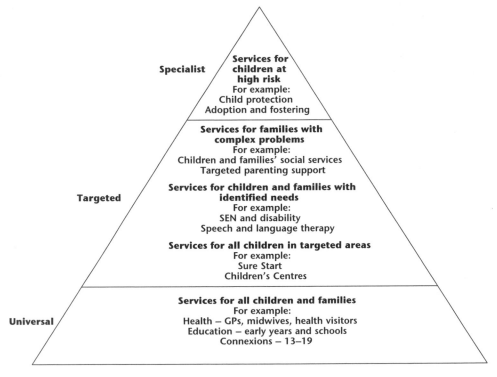

**Figure 2.1:** Targeted services within a universal context
*Source:* DfES (2003a: 21)

For professionals working with children, the report identifies that they may have 'no routine training in child development, child protection or domestic violence issues ... mental health, special educational needs ... ' (DfES 2003a: 22). As an early years professional, covering all aspects of supporting young children, and knowing about their difficulties and areas of development can be overwhelming. A desire to know how to support children and families, as well as ensure education for groups of young children, requires a number of ways of being aware of developments in the field. Sometimes practice may result in being at the 'cutting edge' of ways of working with other professionals and families, particularly in engaging parents in reflecting on practice.

There may be a number of inbuilt checks within settings and specific statutory guidelines that need to be adhered to. At the same time, there will need to be flexibility within that to develop your own way of working with others and also understanding your own practice. Making judgements about what is considered to be appropriate can be confirmed according to other professionals, in discussions with parents, as well as by monitoring and observing children.

## Policy on developing reflective practice in England

The revised Early Years Foundation Stage (EYFS) (2007) contains areas of learning and development for children aged 0–8 years that use observation and assessment to identify and record children's learning. These are considered to provide a 'key basis for taking forward children's development into Key Stage 1, leading to lasting cognitive and social gains' (DfES 2006: 8). Practitioners are required to provide experiences and support to enable children to 'develop a positive sense of themselves and of others' (DfES 2006: 27). The six areas of learning for the EYFS alongside four aspects of *Birth to Three Matters* (Sure Start Unit 2002) interlink within the context of the outcomes for *Every Child Matters* (DfES 2003a) (Figure 2.2 overleaf).

The EYFS consultation document sets out requirements for settings to be able to implement the six different areas of learning and development. These are: physical development; creative development; personal, social and emotional development; communication, language and literacy; problem solving, reasoning and numeracy; knowledge and understanding of the world. The consultation document indicates that practitioners should be:

- planning activities
- developing teamwork
- encouraging children to learn
- developing a constructive relationship with them

**Figure 2.2:** Six areas of learning
*Source:* DfES (2006: 26)

- identifying a key person
- providing time and opportunities for children to learn
- providing opportunities to observe children and develop training to improve practice
- providing a wide range of activities within the outdoor and internal environment
- providing resources for children to learn
- providing time for children to explore in a creative way
- providing opportunities for children to express their ideas.

Perhaps the most significant of all these is the development of teamwork. As early years practitioners, participating in certain enterprises, such as planning activities, will be shaped by knowledge about ways children learn, and different pedagogical approaches. Working with others in a 'planning' context may mean negotiating with the children and, as has been discussed in this chapter, parents, together with other professionals.

## Working with other professionals

Being able to liaise with other professionals, as well as communicating effectively with parents and planning children's activities are key roles of the early years professional. Teamwork includes both a clear distinction between the different roles of professionals, such as key workers, that works along a 'continuum of coordination' (DfES 2003b). This continuum moves from networking to coordination and then cooperation to collaboration. Collaboration includes all aspects of practice along the continuum, including the sharing of information, altering activities to achieve a common purpose, formal links and working together for mutual benefit (DfES 2003b: 23). The key worker may be involved in the initial assessment of the child, and for some children an assessment may result in a statement of their 'special educational needs'. Working with 'outside' agencies as well as parents is particularly relevant to the professional who has responsibility for children with learning difficulties or disabilities (this could also be 'special educational needs coordinator', learning support coordinator, or lead professional in an early years or school setting). One way in which such children may be supported is through early intervention programmes and 'family centred services'. Parents are encouraged to be involved in developing their children's learning, with support from professional services. 'Early intervention' or family-centred educational support for young children with learning difficulties or disabilities is considered to be a cornerstone of the government's strategy for children with 'special educational needs' (DfES 2004a). It is a part of a generalized reform of children's services as set out in the Green Paper *Every Child Matters* (DfES 2003a). The strategy for children with special educational needs also emphasizes, alongside inclusive practice, raising expectations and achievement, the improvement of partnerships with parents, as well as with other professionals. The report specifies the importance of better information sharing and assessments between professionals (from health, education and social care) around the needs of children and their families, leading to early intervention (DfES 2004a: 10).

Sure Start initiatives are also emphasized, such as the Early Support Programme, which was set up to improve services for babies and very young disabled children and their families (DfES 2004b: 12). The report *Together from the Start* (DfES 2003b) outlines one project that could be considered to be family-centred practice as it supports children and parents in their local community and involves teamwork with parents and professionals. In Nottingham city in England, a Portage team (a programme of individualized learning support for young children) organized parent groups based on the Hanen programme (a Canadian programme that supports parents to develop and extend their communication skills with children who have autistic spectrum disorders). The joint training involved a Portage worker and a speech and language therapist. This course of 12 evening sessions brought together parents to discuss video recordings of parents interacting at home with their children. Parents are given the opportunity to meet other professionals who may be involved in their child's future education, and to ask questions and network within the education system (DfES 2003b: 33). The teamwork between professionals could be considered to be a part of the development of a community of practitioners, in so far as a team of professionals and their services are centred around supporting the child and family. The reorganization and integration of health, education and social services in most areas in England into Children's Trusts, will have linked together multi-disciplinary, and multi-agency teams to develop a child-centred and family-friendly approach (Figure 2.3).

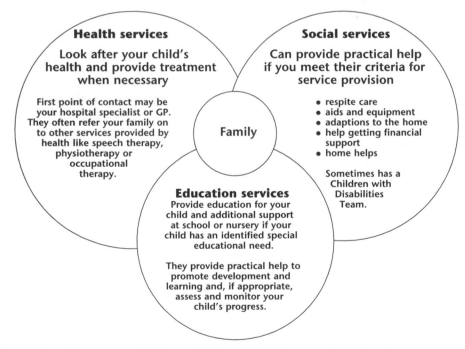

**Figure 2.3: The responsibilities of different services at a local level**
*Source: DfES (2004b: 4)*

While a 'key person' may be responsible for liaising between the professionals and the parents, inter-professional working requires specific ways of working in order to be successful, as Beveridge (2005) notes: 'There is a need for a shared sense of purpose and goals, and a knowledge and understanding of what each has to offer in order to fulfil these. This in turn requires clarity about boundaries and overlaps between each other's roles and responsibilities, and a preparedness for responsive communication based on reciprocal trust and respect for each other's contribution' (Beveridge 2005: 4).

While the role of the child as active contributor may not be directly built into the perception of the 'team', there is evidence of the benefits for children when they participate in decisions related to service provision. Beveridge notes that children must be viewed as key contributors to the development of constructive home–school liaison, and thus, we would argue, to effective reflective practice. Young children's perspectives could be collated through methods adopted in the Mosaic Approach (Clark 2004) and, at the minimum level, by recognizing the child by using their name in any written reports relating to their learning (DfES 2003b). Prichard and Stanton (1999: 653) have identified that effective team performance can be maintained through use of Belbin's (2006) five principles within each team. These consist of:

1. a clear set of team objectives to be performed by each team member, whose status will depend on their (a) professional knowledge and (b) individual way of interacting within a team
2. a balance of team members and roles in relation to the task required
3. a recognition of how each team member can contribute to the team
4. some team members being more able to carry out certain tasks
5. a range of different team members with different types of expertise.

Belbin's taxonomy of team roles identifies a range of characteristics that need to be combined with others for maximum effectiveness when people work together. He argues, as do others who specialize in such personality mapping, that they need to be 'balanced' in terms of the roles of the members.

In practice, teams that come together by chance rather than design in relation to personality, and that include voluntary and other participants such as parents and children, may experience imbalance in strengths and talents. In addition, for those working in more isolated ways (for example, childminders or nannies, or those working in a more ad hoc way) the development of teamwork is more challenging, but nevertheless possible – and desirable when it comes to reflecting on practice. Whether a community of practice is established on an informal basis (for example, a regular meet-up in the park, or at one childminder's home) or a formal one (for example, through studying in a higher education institution where opportunities are given to reflect formally on practice), in today's policy climate, conscious attention to teamwork in relation to how reflective practice is developing, is vitally important for the development of early years provision.

## Conclusion

The external agenda in England increasingly expects that early years professionals should be trained to the level of a pedagogue as in other European countries. The Foundation Stage curriculum, emergent at the time of writing, illustrates an increased commitment towards the early years professional and the knowledge-based curriculum for children aged 0–5 years (DfES 2007). Early years professionals are also considered to need to lead practice across this Early Years Foundation Stage, as well as support and mentor other practitioners, and 'model the skills and behaviours that safeguard and promote good outcomes for children' (CWDC 2006: 5). Muijs *et al.* (2004) note the significance of the development of a workforce of early childhood professionals who need to take on roles of responsibility within their workplace. In particular, the training of this workforce has been found to have an impact on the academic outcomes for children, creating for instance settings with a language-rich environment, sensitive teachers and child-focused communication with the child's home. Integral to developing and sustaining effective practice, reflection on practice is a vital process.

In this chapter, some examples of professionals reflecting on practice and their own experiences have been considered. We have outlined how professionals can reflect on their own experiences, carry out research methods that support reflection and use the information to develop and change their own practice, and we have explored ways in which others, including parents, need to and can be involved in this endeavour.

## References

Arnold, C. (2003) Sharing ideas with parents about key child development concepts, in M. Whalley (ed.) *Involving Parents in their Children's Learning*. London: Paul Chapman.

Bain, J., Ballantyne, R., Packer, J. and Mills, C. (1999) Using journal writing to enhance student teachers' reflectivity during field experience placements, *Teachers and Teaching*, 5: 51–73.

Belbin, M. (2006) *Management Teams, Why They Succeed or Fail*. London: Elsevier.

Beveridge, S. (2005) *Children, Families and Schools, Developing Partnerships for Inclusive Education*. Oxford: Routledge Falmer.

Booth., T. and Ainscow, M. (2004) *Index for Inclusion (Early Years and Childcare)*. Bristol: Centre for Studies in Education.

Chak, A. (2006) Dialogue on 'reflecting on the self', *Reflective Practice*, 7(1), February: 55–57.

Clark, A. (2004) The Mosaic approach and research with young children, in Lewis, V., *et al.* (eds) *The Reality of Research with Children and Young People*. London: Sage.

CWD (2006) http://www.cwdcouncil.org.uk/projects/index.htm (accessed 14 June 2007).

Department for Education and Skills (DfES) (2003a) *Every Child Matters*. Nottingham: DfES.

Department for Education and Skills (DfES) (2003b) *Together from the Start – Practical Guidance for Professionals Working with Disabled Children (Birth to Third Birthday) and their Families*. Nottingham: DfES.

Department for Education and Skills (DfES) (2004a) *Removing Barriers to Achievement: The Government's Strategy for SEN*. Nottingham: DfES.

Department for Education and Skills (DfES) (2004b) *Early Support Family Pack*. Nottingham: DfES.

Department for Education and Skills (DfES) (2006) *Early Years Foundation Stage Consultation Document*, Nottingham: DfES.

Department for Education and Skills (DfES) (2007) *Early Years Foundation Stage*. Nottingham: DfES.

Devereux, J. and Paige-Smith, A. (2004) *Draft Report on the Experiences of Students Studying 'Working with Children in the Early Years'*, Buckingham: Open University.

Goffman, E. (1959) *The Presentation of the Self in Everyday Life*, London: Penguin.

Laevers, F. (1997) *A Process-Oriented Child Follow Up System for Young Children*. Leuven: Centre for Experiential Education.

Muijs, D., Aubrey, C., Harris, A. and Briggs, M. (2004) How do they manage? A review of the research on leadership in early childhood, *Journal of Early Childhood Research*, 2(2): 157–169.

Paige-Smith, A. (1996) Seeing off cuts: researching a professional and parents' campaign to save inclusive education in a London borough, in C. O'Hanlon (ed.) *Professional Development through Action Research in Educational Settings*. London: Falmer Press.

Paige-Smith, A. and Rix, J. (2006) Parents' perceptions and children's experiences of early intervention – inclusive practice? *Journal of Research in Special Educational Needs*, 6: 92–98.

Prichard, J. and Stanton, S. (1999) Testing Belbin's team role theory of effective groups, *Journal of Management Development*, 18(8): 652–665.

Pugh, G. (1989) Parents and professionals in pre-school services: is partnership possible? in S. Wolfendale (ed.) *Parental Involvement*. London: Cassell Educational Ltd.

Rosenstein, B. (2002) The sorcerer's apprentice and the reflective practitioner, *Reflective Practice*, 3(3): 255–261.

Schön, D. (1983) *The Reflective Practitioner*. New York: Basic Books.

Sure Start Unit (2002) *Birth to Three Matters: A Framework to Support Children in their Earliest Years*. London: DfES.

Tait, C. (2003) Getting to know the families, in M. Whalley (ed.) *Involving Parents in their Children's Learning*. London: Paul Chapman Publishing Ltd.

Thompson, K. (2006) *The Cultural World of Professional Practice with Families of Children with a Disability: A New Understanding of Family Centred Practice*. Unpublished PhD thesis, University of Sydney, Australia.

Van Manen, M. (1977) Linking ways of knowing with ways of being practice, *Curriculum Inquiry*, 6: 205–228.

# 3 Exploring leadership: roles and responsibilities of the early years professional

## Linda Pound

Everyone who works in early childhood care and education must demonstrate many of the capabilities and characteristics of a leader. In this chapter the roles and responsibilities of early years professionals are examined and linked with the characteristics of effective leadership. Ways in which practitioners can develop both personally and professionally, through formal and informal approaches, are explored.

## What are the roles and responsibilities of an early years professional?

Early years professionals have a number of different and overlapping roles. Some roles have specific titles – you may, for example, be a teacher, practitioner, assistant, pedagogue, key person or inclusion manager. But, whatever your title, the roles (and their accompanying responsibilities) will undoubtedly overlap with those of colleagues with different titles but often similar roles. The CWDC (www.cwdcouncil.org.uk) identifies a range of roles that early years practitioners undertake:

- graduate level managers (Level 6) and leaders, including those who have gained or are working towards the National Professional Qualification in Integrated Centre Leadership (NPQICL)
- early years professionals who take responsibility for leading and managing the play, care and learning environment
- supervisory staff with responsibility for coordinating various aspects of early years work, including in some situations taking on a management role
- qualified teachers and school support staff whose training or experience may have focussed on early years education
- a wider team of skilled and committed people who take on a range of responsibilities relating to the smooth operation of an early years

setting, including home-based settings and children's education and care.

Everyone involved in the care and education of young children and their families will inevitably take on a vast number of roles (and accompanying responsibilities). In this chapter some aspects of the roles of teacher, pedagogue, key person and leader will be considered.

## Teaching as a role

The government has suggested that there is no real difference between care and education. In terms of children's experience the two are inseparable if high-quality care and education are to be maintained. However, differences continue to be perceived by those involved in different fields. One barrier rests with differing terms and conditions of employment, but a major problem in integrating the two roles of carer and educator lies in the way in which the word 'teaching' is understood. For many lay people, the word 'teacher' conjures up the figures seen in comics: cane-waving, angry or sarcastic individuals. Such images – whether based on actual experience or stereotyped cultural views – do not sit comfortably with the nurturing, caring image required of those working with young children and their families. In fact, they do not sit comfortably with supporting learning effectively at any age.

Over the past ten years, there has developed a greatly increased understanding of the importance of emotional factors in learning and education. This is in large part due to the research and writings of Howard Gardner (1993, 1999) and Joseph LeDoux (1998), the work of both of whom has been made accessible and popularized in the writing of Daniel Goleman (1996). Their findings, supported by the work of many other theorists, have underlined the view of early childhood specialists that teaching is a much more complex matter than simply passing on facts.

Because our experience of being taught and the popular images of teachers that may sometimes be negative, we have to try to put aside these ideas and think about what adults must do to support learning. It is no accident that, in many languages, the same word is used for 'teaching' and 'learning'. In fact, we cannot really claim that we have taught something if it has not been learnt! Teaching has been identified as 'systematically helping children to learn so that they are helped to make connections in their learning and are actively led forward, as well as helped to reflect on what they have already learnt' (QCA 2000: 22).

Effective teaching (which genuinely supports learning) has been said (Jones and Pound, in preparation) to have the following characteristics:

- stimulation that sustains and extends children's interests
- interaction that includes understanding and playing with children
- partnership with parents, together modelling learning and problem solving
- rich language use and a wide range of communicative strategies to support thinking
- the introduction of challenging activities and experiences
- demonstrating skills and knowledge at a time or stage when children can learn from them
- efficient organization of resources, time and space.

# The role of the pedagogue

Widespread discomfort with the term 'teacher' in the early years community has perhaps led to increased use of the term 'pedagogy'. The DfES funded a research project into Effective Pedagogy in the Early Years (REPEY). The research team (Siraj-Blatchford *et al.* 2002: 10) defined pedagogy as:

> refer[ring] to the instructional techniques and strategies which enable learning to take place. It refers to the interactive process between teacher and learner, and it is also applied to include the provision of some aspects of the learning environment (including the concrete learning environment, and the actions of the family and community ... ).

However, this definition does not entirely match up to the way in which the term is more generally used in Europe where the word pedagogy is in more common usage. Collins *et al.* (2001) underline the fact that it is not a term much used in English. They suggest that pedagogy includes evaluation of practice – identifying appropriate and inappropriate approaches to learning and teaching – and understanding of children's development.

Peter Moss has written widely about pedagogues and pedagogy. In his work, he has studied widely practices in a number of European countries and in New Zealand. For Moss (e.g. Moss 2004), a pedagogue takes a holistic view of development, in which learning, care and upbringing are of equal value. In his view, which is based on a number of international studies, well-qualified staff are able to combine these elements to improve the quality of experience for the child. You might say that he sees wiping noses as an integral part of education.

## The role of the key person

Elfer *et al.* (2003: 48, citing Manning-Morton and Thorp 2001) identify a list of tasks or roles that a key person working with children under 3 years of age needs to undertake if they are to meet the full implication of their responsibilities. The list includes the need for key persons to develop trusting relationships with children and parents; interacting with children in ways that build on their preferences and ensure that they feel safe enough to explore the world around them; acknowledging all their feelings, including those that are seen as negative; settling children gently and being with them at key points (e.g. eating, toileting); and seeking support to ensure that the key workers' emotional needs are also addressed.

This range of responsibilities indicates just how complex the role of a key person is. It involves taking a high level of responsibility for all aspects of the children's development and well-being. Manning-Morton and Thorp (2003) point out that taking on this role has a large measure of potential for conflict with parents, particularly in areas such as messy play, potty training and sleeping routines. This is perhaps inevitable in part given the intimate and emotive nature of many of these tasks.

## Leadership roles

Many early years professionals would reject any suggestion that they are leaders. This may in part be because the style of leadership generally adopted in early childhood settings is in sharp contrast to the macho style of leadership demonstrated in popular TV programmes such as *The Apprentice*, or the stereotypical strict and uncaring boss so frequently represented in fictional accounts. Most leaders in the care and education of young children are women and, as Rodd (2006: 23) suggests, women tend to avoid roles that 'involve authority and power'. Many writers (see, for example, Coleman 2002) suggest that although women tend to have a distinctive style of leadership, this does not mean that all women leaders are, say, collaborative; nor does it mean that men are not. Coleman (2002) indicates that when men are leading in fields that are dominated by women, they tend to adopt approaches that are stereotypically attributed to women.

This is probably particularly true in the field of early childhood care and education, which is described as one of the 'caring professions'. Men or women who choose to work with very young children are unlikely to have a view of relationships in which power and authority are paramount. In the first place, babies and toddlers are not easy to manage if an authoritarian style is adopted – they respond better to love and persuasion. Second, anyone seeking power is unlikely to choose a field of work that has such universally low status. So, it would appear that early childhood practitioners avoid a label that they feel does not sit comfortably with their professional identity.

Despite what is an undoubted resistance to taking on the label of leader, early childhood professionals (often without a management 'hat') do in fact have to adopt many of the roles that leaders take on. Early childhood practitioners have to exercise a great deal of independence (Rodd 2006), which people entering other professions, and at a similar stage in their career, would not be expected to demonstrate. Responsible as they are for large numbers of young and vulnerable children, they must frequently make snap decisions about situations, which cannot wait for advice or guidance from others. This means that they must understand how to manage or influence groups, be confident about their ability to make decisions and have a range of skills that will enable them to act wisely and authoritatively. Of course, the setting or centre will have policies in place to guide decision-making but young children, and their families who may be under stress, may act unpredictably.

Working with young children is of course pleasurable and rewarding but it carries enormous responsibilities for everyone undertaking the work. This is one of the major reasons why reflection on leadership is of such vital importance in early years work – when team members are treated with respect and empathy they are much more likely to treat children in this way too (Pound and Joshi 2005). This underlines the notion that effective leadership is heavily dependent on good relationships within a team. Put another way, leaders exercise leadership through their relations with other people: leadership is a *relational* activity. The process of reflection is vital to effective curriculum planning, sound assessment of children's development and progress, constructive and consistent relations within teams, and genuine partnership with parents and community. Each one of these activities demands of an early years professional a highly professional thoughtful review or evaluation of key issues during the working day.

Another characteristic of the work of early years professionals is that practitioners need to operate in a variety of teams – sometimes as a leader, sometimes as a team member. Early childhood settings are extremely complex and almost everyone involved finds themselves undertaking a wide range of roles. Edgington (2004: 15) makes the point that this can give you 'some insight into what it feels like to be led, which you can relate to feelings of the people you lead'. It is beyond dispute that an effective leader needs to be a good communicator, but it is also clear that some team members can make it difficult to communicate (which must by definition be a two-way process) by closing down the channels of communication (Pound and Joshi 2005). Similarly, the leader's role of delegating must, to be effective, be met with a willingness to take responsibility and to be reliable.

In addition, practitioners who have chosen to work with young children find themselves becoming closely involved with parents and community – areas of work that require a wide range of additional skills and knowledge. This highlights a further factor in leadership in this sector, which is the sheer complexity of the relationships that form part of the work. The multi-professional work that is required in multi-function or integrated centres requires leaders to take account of the different training, experience, assumptions, expectations and practices within the staff team. This demands such 'leaderful' (Raelin 2003) characteristics as flexibility, liaising with community, collaborating with others and a sense of compassion.

Raelin's words on compassionate leadership (2003: 16) sum up well the qualities that early years professionals, whether or not they are designated leaders, bring to leadership:

> By demonstrating compassion, one extends unadulterated commitment to preserving the dignity of others ... each member of the community is valued regardless of his or her background or social standing, and all viewpoints are considered regardless of whether they conform to current thought processes. In practicing [*sic*] compassion, leaders take the stance of a learner who sees the adaptability of the community as dependent upon the contribution of others. Members of the community, not necessarily the position leaders, handle problems as they arise. Compassionate leaders recognize that values are intrinsically interconnected with leadership and that there is no higher value than democratic participation.

Another theory that adds credibility to the notion of early years professionals as leaders, no matter what their designation, is the idea of 'distributed leadership' (Gronn 2003), which is seen as increasingly important. Many organisations (including schools, children's centres and many other settings involved in the care and education of young children) are too complex to be in the hands of a single leader, and many people – often in small and apparently insignificant ways, provide leadership of different kinds, and perhaps different styles. In many walks of life, including the care and education of young children, many people have to operate as leaders; it cannot all be left to the person at the top.

This is not to suggest that designated leaders are redundant (although in some community ventures there is an entirely flat management structure). What is vital, however, is that in the same way as pedagogues and teachers have a range of strategies for managing groups and situations, so leaders need a range of styles. Although leaders may claim (or be categorized as having) a particular style, that style may not or need not be fixed, and it may be helpful if the leadership style can be changed to suit circumstances. Rodd (2006), for example, suggests that a young or inexperienced team may benefit from a directive style of leadership, while teams where there is a high degree of conflict might be improved by a more democratic style of leadership. Goleman *et al.* (2002: 55) echo this view when they suggest that visionary leaders are needed when 'changes require a new vision or when a clear direction is needed'. Similarly, while we may not always think of *commanding leadership* (or being very direct in telling people what to do) as an empowering style, it may help in situations where, say, change is proving difficult. It is, however, generally believed that effective organizations adopt empowering leadership styles at every tier or level of responsibility.

Childminders and nannies, and other professionals who generally work alone, can also demonstrate leadership qualities. This may be within a community group or network, or even at informal gatherings. One mark of a leader is their ability to influence decisions in situations where they may have no real power but where their authority and credibility, or perhaps their ability to put forward clear and believable arguments, enables them to control outcomes. The teamwork that exists between parents and carers, however, does not ideally have a leader since it is said that the adults work in partnership. There will, of course, be situations in which one takes a lead or influences the other.

Owen (2005) makes an interesting distinction between effective emerging and experienced leaders. He suggests that effective experienced leaders exhibit a range of characteristics or skills, many of which mirror the characteristics that early years professionals must employ in their day-to-day work:

- build commitment
- influence and motivate others
- create a leadership team
- manage conflict and crises well
- are decisive but 'embrace ambiguity'
- show honesty and integrity
- seek to improve their own competence and that of others.

## Tasks, roles and responsibilities

It may be helpful at this point to highlight the differences between tasks, roles and responsibilities. The tasks that early years professionals with apparently different roles take on may look very similar: they are likely to be engaged in conversations with parents; to spend time interacting with children or involved in their personal care; and to undertake housekeeping tasks. Their reasons for taking on these tasks will be underpinned by the responsibilities they feel they have. So what are the responsibilities of early years professionals? To whom are they accountable?

## Accountable to children?

There can be no doubt that early years professionals are responsible for children. They must regularly act *in loco parentis*. However, being responsible or accountable to children is a rather different matter. The former often relies heavily on health and safety – keeping children safe from risk and harm. The agenda set out in *Every Child Matters* (DfES 2003) ensures that all professionals are in no doubt as to the nature of their responsibilities to children. The relevant legislation requires early years professionals to demonstrate their attempts to ensure that children adopt healthy lifestyles, feel safe and adopt safe practices, enjoy their education, make a positive contribution to the community, and prepare for their future economic well-being. In order to aid reflection on the difference between the two types of responsibility, it may be useful to consider an illustrative issue.

Awareness of their responsibility for children may lead some practitioners to avoid risk. Children who are physically fearful have insufficient experience and will not have developed the necessary strategies to keep themselves safe. A desire to maintain responsibility for a child may lead us to overlook our larger responsibility for their general well-being and development.

There is a strong and current interest in listening to children, in seeking their views. Clark and Moss (2001) remind us that listening brings responsibilities, since as we build relationships with children and come to understand them better we have a responsibility to act on our new insights. Practitioners have, in short, a moral and professional responsibility to act on what they have found out. This in turn means that roles become changed or modified. We may, for example, develop as researchers, or we may change the way we interact with parents or with colleagues.

## Accountable to families?

Part of a practitioner's responsibility for children's development is a responsibility to work in partnership with parents. Failure to do this can place unnecessary and unhelpful pressure on the children themselves (Pound 2006). The term 'partnership' is widely used but means many different things to different people. It may be salutary to professionals to turn the phrase 'partnership with parents' on its head and consider how the meaning is changed if we say instead 'partnership with professionals' (Langford and Weissbourd 1997: 153).

Pen Green Centre in Corby is widely acknowledged to have developed firm partnerships with parents. Margy Whalley set up the centre and is now the director of the research centre that has been established there. She has written widely about partnership (Whalley 2001: 9) and suggests that professionals have the following responsibilities.

- *Exemplify good practice:* parents expect that professionals will do their best for their children but, as Manning-Morton and Thorp (2001) point out, their expectations do not always coincide, either with each other or with professionals. This means that professionals must be ready to model, explain and justify their practice while trying to understand parents' concerns.
- *Provide information about current research:* providing not only information about research but opportunities to understand the implications.
- *Offer appropriate parent education and professional support:* the staff team at Pen Green is particularly proactive and effective in supporting parents in developing their knowledge and understanding of child development.
- *Help parents to develop and sustain their sense of self-esteem and self-efficacy:* Manning-Morton and Thorp (2003: 152) echo this view when they suggest that practitioners need to examine the attitudes they hold towards families. Langford and Weissbourd (1997) identify the possibility that a barrier to full participation may be low self-esteem or lack of confidence in parents. They go on to suggest that parents should be empowered to be actively involved in governance and that this would involve better training for staff to work on more equal terms with parents. It would also involve increased staffing to cope with the demands of 'a more comprehensive parent-support program' (Langford and Weissbourd 1997: 153).

## Accountable to the community?

The pre-schools of Reggio Emilia, in northern Italy, have been listed among the best schools in the world by *Time* magazine. They also place a strong emphasis on working with parents and community. Parents are identified as partners and 'resource people' (www.sightlines.initiative.com/keyprinciples). A much more strongly worded principle is headed 'Children are Connected' and states: 'The child is a member of a family and a community rather than an isolated individual. The child learns through interaction with peers, adults, objects and symbols. Preschool centres are seen as a system of relations embedded in a wider social system.'

Practitioners in Reggio Emilia have a clear sense of responsibility to the community. Scott (2001: 21) writes of the climate of trust between 'parents, practitioners and policymakers in Reggio Emilia', among whom the way in which they 'listen to each other is actively extended to the children too'. This underlines an important aspect of responsibility or accountability, which is that there is a strong element of reciprocity. The practitioners feel responsible or answerable to the community including parents and policy-makers but the members of the community also have an overwhelming sense of responsibility to provide the best they can for the children of the community. This includes creating good working conditions for practitioners since they believe that the self-esteem, which comes from comfortable and attractive working environments, has an impact on the self-esteem and well-being of children.

Amid all the praise for this work, a word of caution is needed. The work there is undoubtedly impressive but, as Moss (2001: 133) reminds us, ideas and approaches that work within one community do not readily transfer directly into another. He draws attention to the political and economic climate there and concludes:

> For those of us who live and work in very different contexts, Reggio provides us with a sort of lens for looking at our own situations – in Britain, Sweden, the USA, or wherever – a lens which helps to make the invisible visible and to see what is visible in a different light. This can enable us to become more critical thinkers.

## Accountable to society?

The government's childcare agenda designed to support working parents has given practitioners an increased measure of responsibility for parents and families. Making provision for children that allows parents to get to work on time can shape the way in which the setting is organized. Of course, childminders and nannies have always carried responsibilities of this sort but for many practitioners this is an entirely new experience. This could be interpreted as a societal responsibility but what is more often intended when this area of responsibility is raised is the issue of accountability.

The introduction of the National Curriculum, the development of SATs and other testing procedures, and the creation of Ofsted inspections all occurred in the early 1990s to monitor (on society's behalf) the way in which schools were addressing their responsibilities. These developments were seen by many working in schools as indicating a lack of trust. The trust that has been commented on as being a feature of work in Reggio Emilia seems not to exist in this country. This may, as some suggest, have arisen from media pressure, concerns about unequal levels of achievement, a quest for value for money, a drive for higher levels of accountability across many sectors, or a perceived effort to shift power from teachers to politicians. Which of these factors do you think have influenced shifts in educational policy?

One of the most persistent objections to increased levels of monitoring came from teachers concerned about the erosion of their professionalism. Citing the example of lawyers or doctors, teachers considered that they should be self-monitoring and that the absence of trust eroded their status. They argued that there was no need to impose systems to make them accountable since they, as professionals, were already accountable to children and parents.

## Accountable to the team?

You are likely to be a member of one or more teams. Whether or not you are the leader of a particular team you, as a professional, must take your share of responsibility for the effective working of the team. The work of the team might be focused around meeting the needs of children with special education needs. It might be a class-based team focusing on the needs of one set or cohort of children. Frequently practitioners find themselves in a range of teams – an extended day team, a management group, an action committee and so on. Responsibilities of leaders include both responsibility *to* the team and responsibility *for* the team. If you have a designated leadership role you will have noticed reference in this and preceding sections to the responsibilities you have for the team. You will, for example, need to take a lead in:

- ensuring good relations
- setting a climate in which staff feel valued and strive to keep learning and developing
- identifying and keeping central a set of core values or a vision for the setting
- monitoring and developing the quality of provision.

However, these things cannot be achieved by the leader alone. Goleman *et al.* (2002: 180) give an example of a high-powered leader who starts every meeting by reminding the team that everyone (not just he himself) has to be responsible for:

- keeping us on track if we get off
- facilitating group input
- raising questions about our procedures (e.g. asking the group to clarify where it is going and offering summaries of the issues being discussed to make sure we have a shared understanding of them)

- using good listening skills – either build on the ongoing discussion or clearly signal that we want a change of subject, and ask if that is OK . . .

## The responsibilities of leaders

Although the accountability provided by inspection can sometimes seem removed from day-to-day concerns, the debate focused around *Every Child Matters* (DfES 2003) has sharpened the level of accountability to aspects that clearly impact on children's well-being. In the 2005 version of the Ofsted framework (in England) for nursery and primary schools, self-evaluation forms (SEFs) were introduced as an important step forward in promoting a professional approach to self-assessment. Leaders are asked to take increased responsibility for assessing their own performance.

### Accountable to and for yourself

Current thinking about leadership in integrated centres suggests that the function or purpose of leadership is about transformation (Whalley 2004). Indeed it is thought by some that the whole purpose or function of education is about transformation. Whalley (2004: based on 34, citing Mezirow 1975, 1982) suggests that an approach to leadership that leads to transformation includes:

- self-examination
- exploring options for new ways of acting
- building competence and self-confidence in new roles
- planning a course of action
- acquiring knowledge and skills for implementing one's plans
- provisional efforts to try new roles and to assess feedback.

Becoming a professional is a process. Experience and reflections gradually lead the aspiring professional towards becoming what have been called mature or influential professionals (see Pound, in preparation). The characteristics of these professionals are that they

- have 'long experience in a range of roles and functions'
- 'hold composite, high level, professional leadership roles', and
- 'strive for professional insight, perspective and realism' (Pound, in preparation).

While the first two characteristics cannot readily be put in place without long experience, the third point, about insight, perspective and realism, is an area for which the less experienced and developing early years professional can take responsibility.

One key role for an early years professional in transforming both self and institution lies in exciting the enthusiasm of other practitioners, both within and beyond the team. McGregor (2003: 126) suggests that 'the role of leadership is ... in facilitating engagement, imagination and alignment'. Crompton (1997) suggests that community leadership requires commitment, and Owen (2005) highlights his view that effective emerging leaders focus on '3 Ps': people, positivity and professionalism (including loyalty and reliability).

Achieving this level of transformation and mature professionalism can be supported by a number of formal and informal strategies. In this chapter the focus is on informal approaches. However, such strategies and attendance on a formal course of study will be mutually supportive. Becoming an increasingly reflective practitioner is key to this process of becoming professional. A publication of the Teacher Training Agency (2000, cited in Pollard 2002: 36) suggests that reflective practitioners need to acquire the skills that enable them to:

- identify teaching and learning problems
- weigh up research and evidence objectively
- make the links with classroom practice
- evaluate ways of putting new knowledge and skills to work.

Glover *et al.* (2002: 296) have suggested that formal study enables course participants to acquire a range of qualities that enhance their ability to reflect. They suggest that successful graduates should have:

1. the ability to research, analyse and present information coherently
2. breadth of vision (including the ability to continue learning ... , curiosity about other subject, a breadth of knowledge)
3. expertise in their chosen field, the ability to achieve a balanced view, an open and flexible mind
4. a good knowledge of the English language ... [and]
5. impetus to reach a goal in a disciplined manner.

Reflective practice is the subject of many publications. Bolton (2005) emphasizes the importance of the writing process in aiding reflection for a range of professionals, including those in 'medicine, education, clinical psychology, nursing, therapy and leadership (2005: back cover). Johns (2004: 18), writing primarily for health professionals, offers a number of models to support his own model for structured reflection. He identifies a number of what he terms reflective cues, which include the following.

- Focus on a description of an experience that seems significant in some way.
- What particular issues seem significant to pay attention to?
- How were others feeling and what made them feel that way?
- How was I feeling and what made me feel that way?
- What was I trying to achieve and did I respond effectively?
- What knowledge did or might have informed me?
- How does this situation connect with previous experiences?
- How might I respond more effectively given this situation again?
- What would be the consequences of alternative actions for others and myself?

Observation is an essential element of reflective practice. However, as Drummond (1993) reminds us, looking and listening are not neutral or objective activities. The observer's mind or perception of a situation creates errors in observations, since we may unwittingly distort what we see or hear in line with our prejudgements or prejudices. Indeed, even professional training and experience can lead us to see and interpret in particular ways. Sources of bias may also arise from culture, from language differences, or be based on physical appearance or gender.

Sometimes observations can become formalized and lead us to a form of practitioner or action research. Rodd (1998: 174) comments that 'research is also important for leadership ... because it is a recognised means of gathering the facts and information which carry weight in arguments for change'. Clark and Moss (2001) make the point that research brings responsibilities – meaning that if you have identified problems or issues for the child, then you have a responsibility to act on the knowledge.

*Reflexive* practice – a way of understanding more about practice that is used – should enable the early years professional to stand back from her/his own research, observations or investigations in order to identify the ways in which our perspectives influence our judgements. The term 'reflexive' has been used by Clark and Moss (2001) and they define reflexivity as listening to the voice of the child as an active process involving the interpretation of the data gathered from children. Eide and Winger (2005: 83) demonstrate reflexivity when they suggest that researchers need to bring to their work 'insight, ... knowledge about children and ... the ability to be a humble interpreter reflecting upon the children's statements'. They also write of the importance of 'being a spokesperson for the children ... and constantly wishing to improve'.

## Points for reflection

- What are your key roles and responsibilities?
- Which of these demand leadership qualities?
- To what extent do you feel able to demonstrate 'compassionate leadership' (Raelin 2003)? Are you able to value all members of your professional community – children, parents, staff, partner agencies, etc.?
- How do you address your responsibilities to your team? Are you able to promote good relations, to create a climate in which everyone feels valued, to maintain core values, and to monitor and develop the quality of provision?
- How do you encourage team members to share responsibility for achieving good relations and effective practice?

## References

Bolton, G. (2005) *Reflective Practice* (2nd edn). London: Sage Publications.

Clark, A. and Moss, P. (2001) *Listening to Young Children: The Mosaic Approach*. London: National Children's Bureau.

Coleman, M. (2002) *Women as Headteachers: Striking the Balance*. Stoke-on-Trent: Trentham Books.

Collins, J., Insley, K. and Soler, J. (eds) (2001) *Developing Pedagogy*. London: Paul Chapman Publishing.

Crompton, D. (1997) Community leadership, in S. Kagan and T. Bowman (eds) *Leadership in Early Care and Education*. Washington, DC: National Association for the Education of Young Children.

Department for Education and Skills (DfES) (2003) *Every Child Matters*. Nottingham: DfES.

Drummond, M.-J. (1993) *Assessing Children's Learning*. London: David Fulton Publishers.

Edgington, M. (2004) *The Foundation Stage Teacher in Action*. London: Paul Chapman Publishing.

Eide, B. and Winger, N. (2005) From the children's point of view: methodological and ethical challenges, in A. Clark, A. Kjorholt and P. Moss (eds) *Beyond Listening*. Bristol: The Policy Press.

Elfer, P., Goldschmied, E. and Selleck, D. (2003) *Key Persons in the Nursery*. London: David Fulton Publishers.

Gardner, H. (1993) *Frames of Mind* (2nd edn). London: Fontana.

Gardner, H. (1999) *Intelligence Reframed*. New York: Basic Books.

Glover, D., Law, S. and Youngman, A. (2002) Graduateness and employability: student perceptions of personal outcomes of university education, *Research in Post-Compulsory Education*, 7(3): 293–306.

Goleman, D. (1996) *Emotional Intelligence*. London: Fontana.

Goleman, D., Boyatzis, R. and McKee, A. (2002) *The New Leaders*. London: Little, Brown.

Gronn, P. (2003) *The New Work of Educational Leaders*. London: Sage.

Johns, C. (2004) *Becoming a Reflective Practitioner* (2nd edn). Malden, Surrey: Blackwell Publishing.

Jones, C. and Pound, L. (in preparation) *Leadership and Management in the Early Years: A Practical Guide*. Maidenhead: Open University Press.

Langford, J. and Weissbourd, B. (1997) New directions in parent leadership in a family-support context, in S. L. Kagan and T. Bowman (eds) *Leadership in Early Care and Education*. Washington, DC: National Association for the Education of Young Children (NAEYC).

LeDoux, J. (1998) *The Emotional Brain*. London: Weidenfeld & Nicolson.

Manning-Morton, J. and Thorp, M. (2001) *Key Times: A Framework for Developing High Quality Provision for Children Under Three Years*. London: Camden EYDCP/University of North London.

Manning-Morton, J. and Thorp, M. (2003) *Key Times for Play*. Maidenhead, Berks: Open University Press.

McGregor, J. (2003) Collaboration in communities of practice, in Bennett, N. and Anderson, L. (eds) *Rethinking Educational Leadership*. London: Sage Publications.

Moss, P. (2001) The otherness of Reggio, in L. Abbott and C. Nutbrown (eds) *Experiencing Reggio Emilia – Implications for Pre-School Provision*. Buckingham: Open University Press.

Moss, P. (2004) Getting beyond childcare, quality . . . the Barcelona targets. Paper presented at the Developments about ECEC and Related Policy and Research Conference, 23 November, The Netherlands.

Owen, J. (2005) *How to Lead*. Harlow: Pearson Education Ltd.

Pollard, A. (ed.) (2002) *Readings for Reflective Teaching*. London: Continuum.

Pound, L. and Joshi, U. (2005) Management, teamwork and leadership, in L. Dryden, R. Forbes, P. Mukherji and L. Pound (eds) *Essential Early Years*. London: Hodder Arnold.

Pound, L. (2006) *Ocean Mathematics Project Evaluation of Foundation Stage Pilot Project 2005–6*. Unpublished report.

Pound, L. (in preparation) Leadership in the early years, in L. Miller and C. Cable (eds) *Professionalism in the Early Years*. London: Hodder/Arnold.

Qualifications and Curriculum Authority (QCA) (2000) *Curriculum Guidance for the Foundation Stage*. London: DfES/QCA.

Raelin, J. (2003) *Creating Leaderful Organizations*. San Francisco: Berrett-Koehler.

Rodd, J. (1998) *Leadership in Early Education* (2nd edn). Buckingham: Open University Press.

Rodd, J. (2006) *Leadership in Early Education* (3rd edn). Maidenhead: Open University Press.

Scott, W. (2001) Listening and learning, in L. Abbott and C. Nutbrown (eds) *Experiencing Reggio Emilia – Implications for Pre-School Provision*. Buckingham: Open University Press.

Siraj-Blatchford, I., Sylva, K., Muttock, S., Gilden, R. and Bell, D. (2002) *Researching Effective Pedagogy in the Early Years*. London: Institute of Education/Dept of Educational Studies, Oxford.

Whalley, M. (2001) *Involving Parents in their Children's Learning*. London: Paul Chapman Publishing.

Whalley, M. for the National College for School Leadership (NCSL) (2004) *Participants' Guide: Book 6 'Developing the Practitioner Researcher Research Stages 1–8' National Professional Qualification in Integrated Centre Leadership*. Nottingham: NCSL.

# PART 2

# How does reflective practice inform working with children?

# Introduction to Part 2

**Alice Paige-Smith and Anna Craft**

In this part of the book we consider areas of children's learning in order to support their well-being and develop a holistic approach within the early years curriculum. The four chapters focus on areas of pedagogy and professional development common across the early years curriculum and also span the external expectations for early years professionals. The authors exemplify current practice as well as the underpinning theoretical approaches to the different areas of children's learning in the early years within the notion of the competent child. The areas explored in Part 2 include creativity, inclusive education, parental involvement, multi-disciplinary working and children's emotional development. The discussions are applicable to a range of early years settings, spanning the age range 0–8 years.

# 4   Children's social and emotional development

## Naima Browne

This chapter explores children's emotional development from a perspective that emphasizes the importance of practitioners considering identity, equity and children's rights as key issues offering material for practitioners to reflect on together. This chapter will look at the ways in which children's identities and sense of who they are develop within a social context. The relationship between children's growing identities and their emotional well-being is explored. The impact of factors such as gender and culture on children's identities and emotional development is also be examined. The chapter will look at transitions in relation to young children's emotional development. Recent research into the impact of transition will be discussed. The important role that listening to children plays in supporting their emotional development is briefly discussed, although the issue of listening to children is covered in depth in later chapters.

## Introduction

Practitioners must provide experiences and support to enable children to develop a positive sense of themselves and of others. They must support children's emotional well-being, helping them to know themselves and what they can do. They must also help children to develop respect for others, social skills and a positive disposition to learn. (DfES 2006: Section 3.9)

Social and emotional development involves, among other things, a growing understanding of how to behave in different situations, the ability to empathize with others, to be self-controlled and develop positive dispositions towards learning. Young children's emotional and social development includes developing good interpersonal skills, developing positive relationships with others, developing intra-personal understandings, and growing self-confidence and self-esteem. A child's emotional and social development is also inextricably linked with their growing sense of who they are: their personal identity.

## Emotional well-being and resilience

Thinking about emotional well-being may help us as practitioners to think more broadly about emotional development. This concept is increasingly being used: 'Considering children's emotional and social development is clearly an important aspect of professional practice and recent research would suggest that in the foundation stage children's emotional health is becoming a priority in local authorities across England' (Ofsted 2007).

Children's emotional and social development is shaped and influenced by a wide range of factors. A child's early experiences of interactions with others, for example, helps lay the foundations for future relationships and the child's ongoing emotional development. Children's diverse life experiences and how they are related to in different ways by other children and by their parents also set up expectations about their behaviour and their emotional development, and reveal what their parents and others think is 'typical' and acceptable.

## Developmental psychology and patterns of emotional development

Practitioners working in the UK, USA and north European settings are used to working within the developmental psychology discourse. This means that practitioners tend to think about children's development in terms of ages, stages and identified markers or milestones of progress and development.

Piaget's work has been hugely influential in the field of early years, not least in terms of presenting the child as learning and developing 'naturally' and progressing through a series of clearly identifiable, universal stages on the journey to adult modes of thinking and behaving. Piaget's findings have been criticized by psychologists such as Donaldson (1978) and Hughes (1986), whose research suggested that young children were able to demonstrate far more sophisticated levels of thinking than Piaget had claimed. Nonetheless, the notion of the naturally developing child remains a very powerful concept for early years practitioners. Comments made by early years practitioners and parents, such as 'What stage is she at?', reveal how this particular view of the child is still firmly established within the early years field.

The ideas of Vygotsky and Bruner led to social constructivism being incorporated into the dominant discourse on early years learning; both emphasized that learning is socially situated. While most practitioners acknowledge the importance of social interaction there has not, however, been a move away from envisaging children's learning in terms of ages and stages. This is evident in guidance provided for settings (e.g. QCA 2000).

The notion that children's learning and development can be quantified, measured and tested is related to the concept of childhood as a 'stage' in human development. In this particular model of human development the desirable end state is seen to be adulthood. In societies where adulthood and childhood are seen as stages and states, adulthood is seen to be the last stage in development, or the 'end state'. Adults come to possess 'adult' characteristics through an unvarying and universal developmental process.

The distinction between childhood and adulthood may seem to be obvious and 'natural' but while the concept of adulthood as a state predominates in western societies, in many other societies adulthood is seen as a process: adults are continually developing and therefore never reach complete maturity (Archard 1993). Archard's analysis of different perceptions of childhood and adulthood shows that conceptions of childhood are socially constructed. Once we begin to accept that 'childhood' is socially constructed and what it consists of will vary from culture to culture we also need to question the validity of the idea of the 'naturally developing child' who passes through universal developmental stages.

The developmental stages and markers evident in official guidance such as the *Curriculum Guidance for the Foundation Stage* (QCA 2000) have arisen from a wide range of research findings over the years. The research has focused on what children seem to understand or can do at various ages and stages with little attention given to the children's real-life experiences as active members of their communities and wider society. The result is that 'the child' in developmental psychology is, in a sense, a synthesis of all the children researched. This synthetic or fabricated child, the child against whom children in settings are measured, is not a real child but only signifies the 'norm' or what is seen by research to be 'typical'. Factors such as culture and gender have been rendered invisible by the distillation process. No child matches this 'typical' child but some children's development will be more 'typical' than others.

The concept of the 'naturally developing' child masks the ways in which culture has an impact on the nature of children's life experiences, the ways in which these life experiences are interpreted by the child and the impact of these experiences on the child's development. Erica Burman, who has looked closely at ideas and assumptions underpinning developmental psychology, has argued that developmental psychologists studying infant behaviour have tended to focus on what is measurable. In Burman's words they have tended to suppress 'the indeterminate, ambiguous, non-instrumental features of infant behaviour' (Burman 1994: 33, cited in Penn 2005: 11). A possible consequence of this is that not only *what* some children learn but also certain life experiences and *how* children learn may have been seen as irrelevant or unimportant by researchers. Failing to take full account of the ways in which diverse experiences and discourses contribute towards children's learning and development leads to differences between children's patterns of development being seen as problematic.

Focusing on sets of measurable outcomes suggests that 'children' are homogenous and those that meet the milestones are fine (i.e. 'normal'), while those that do not are outside the norm and this leads to anxieties about groups of children and individual children who, because of their diverse life experiences, which are influenced by the interaction of race, gender and social class, are not conforming to white, male, middle-class norms of development.

This is important to bear in mind when thinking about young children's social and emotional development as children whose social and emotional development does not seem to match the norm, those who are not 'typical', are seen as different or exceptional, and their development is viewed as a problem that requires attention in order to bring the child's development into the range regarded as 'normal'.

## Culture and emotional development

Emphasising the 'naturalness' of children's development has led to practitioners monitoring and measuring individual children's development to ensure that they do not stray too far from the 'norm', but few questions are asked about the validity of these norms.

Cross-cultural research into patterns of adult–child interaction has revealed that culture has an impact on what parents value in terms of their child's emotional development (Commons and Miller 1998). According to Levine et al. (1994) parental goals vary in different cultures. In some cultures (e.g. the USA and the UK) Levine et al. have argued that parents have a pedagogical model of child rearing and one of the characteristics of this model is that parents aim to ensure that their children learn to feel emotionally independent from a relatively young age. This has led to common child-rearing practices such as ensuring babies sleep on their own, rather than with their mother, and also a higher tolerance of babies' crying. For parents from cultures that adopt a paediatric model of child rearing (e.g. Gussii, Kenya) the main focus is on protecting the health and survival of their very young children. This has led to child-rearing practices that include the child sleeping with the mother, rapid responses to a child's crying, and high levels of holding and touching babies and young children.

Commons and Miller (1998) suggest that these different parenting styles may have long-term effects on the emotional development of babies and young children. Early stressful experiences (such as sleeping apart from the mother or being allowed to cry for periods of time) may result in higher levels of the stress hormone cortisol being secreted, which in turn may result in long-term alterations to secretion patterns of cortisol and other stress hormones in later life, which impacts on an individual's ability to handle emotionally difficult situations (Commons and Miller 1998).

Research by Farver and Shin (1997) has also highlighted the probability that culture has an impact on children's social and emotional development. Farver and Shin found that Korean-American children's pretend play themes focused on familiar everyday activities, while Anglo-American children's pretend play themes were based on more fantastic and dangerous subjects. Farver and Shin have argued that the minimal social conflict and familiar scenarios evident in Korean-American children's play themes may reflect the emphasis on 'harmonious interpersonal relationships' that characterizes Korean culture (Farver and Shin 1997: 553). This stands in contrast to the dominant culture of Anglo-American children, which values independence and self-reliance and is then reflected in the play themes through which Anglo-American children pursue their own interests and concerns, even if this involves a degree of conflict. Without acknowledging the impact of culture on children's experiences and learning paths it is probable that many Anglo-American children would be regarded as on track in terms of their developing independence, while their Korean-American peers may be described as needing extra support in this area and may possibly be viewed as a 'disadvantaged' group because their social and emotional development appears to lag behind what is regarded as 'normal' for Anglo-American children of the same age.

The theories arising from cross-cultural research have implications for early years practitioners. Working with families drawn from a diverse range of cultures means that we need to be willing to consider the validity of different ways of caring for young children. We need to acknowledge that it is the dominant educational discourses and culture that determine what counts as 'good practice' rather than universally held ideas about young children's needs. Gussii mothers, for example, watching film of American mothers caring for their babies were very distressed at how long babies, were left to cry before the mothers responded to them (Commons and Miller 1998).

Research findings such as these ought to make practitioners pause and reflect on the extent to which professional practice within their setting and their assessments of children's development indicate an uncritical acceptance of culturally specific ideas about young children's social and emotional development. Is the practice within your setting based on the assumption that the markers and milestones you use are the only way, or even the 'best' way, of supporting and assessing young children's emotional development?

## Identity and self-esteem

In everyday conversation we tend to use the term 'identity' to mean 'who someone is'. Children's identity develops as they interact with others during the course of their lives. This is not to suggest that babies are 'things' rather than people, but rather that our life experiences help shape our view of ourselves and our identities shift and are reconstructed over time. Our sense of self, therefore, is not stable and fixed but changes with experience. Furthermore each of us does not have a unified, single identity but instead we have multiple identities. We have this range of identities because we all adopt a range of roles in the various social contexts within which we operate. These multiple identities emerge as children learn to make sense of social interactions and engage in a range of discourses. Not all these discourses will provide the same world-view and some of them will conflict with each other. A young child may know, for example, 'she is dad's little daughter and she makes him laugh; her baby brother's loving older sister when she cuddles him and gives him his bottle; her older brother's noisy little sister when she dances and sings to his records; and Alison the artist at nursery when her teacher admires her paintings' (Dowling 2000: 2).

There are so many facets to identity that it helps to focus on one when thinking about the process by which children develop their sense of self. In British society knowing whether you are a girl or a boy is deemed to be important. As soon as a child is born the parents are asked whether the new baby is a girl or boy, and as a young baby adults will label the child as a girl or boy: 'Who's a tired boy then?' or 'Aren't you a lovely girl?' The young child is expected to learn whether they themselves are a girl or a boy and also to accurately assign others to one of two categories: male or female. Young children growing up in this and many other societies are introduced to the dominant gender discourse that presents female and male, girl and boy, feminine and masculine as mutually exclusive categories: you are either one or the other, you cannot be both. In this society as a whole the dominant or most widely accepted form of masculinity emphasizes, among other things, competitiveness, physical strength and rationality. This masculinity is complemented by an 'emphasized femininity' that is characterized by 'compliance, nurturance and empathy' (Connell 1987: 187–8, cited in Browne 2004: 69). Children are likely to be exposed to other discourses in which ideas of femininity and masculinity may be different from those presented by the dominant discourse. Children need to actively negotiate these different discourses and make decisions about how they would like to position themselves within them and how they would like others to view them. Operating effectively within the dominant gender discourse means that a child can relate unproblematically and unambiguously, in gender terms, with others. It also tends to attract a positive response from those around the child ('He's a real boy isn't he?' or 'You're such a good girl, so kind'). This means that, for some children, 'correctly' positioning themselves within the dominant gender discourse brings about positive emotional feedback. Other children may choose to adopt a different position.

While young children are active agents in constructing their identity they are still influenced by the opinions and views of others and will be particularly sensitive to the views and opinions of people they are close to (e.g. parents, carers, teachers, friends, siblings). Early years practitioners can enable children to explore and develop their sense of self by encouraging children to explore different 'ways of being'.

Self-identity and self-esteem are closely linked. When children are developing their identity they are learning to see themselves as others see them. Self-esteem is the value placed on one's own identity. Just as self - identities are shifting and changing so too does someone's self-esteem. A child may feel very valued in one context but less so in another. These changes in self-esteem will be related to how others respond to the child. If a child feels that important adults in their lives care about them, value them and accept them as they are, she or he is likely to have a high level of self-esteem. If, on the other hand, adults criticize the child for seeming not to possess characteristics valued by the adults the child is likely to have lower self-esteem. A child's chattiness and lively interaction with adults may be valued at home but these same characteristics may not be viewed so positively in another context (e.g. an early years setting). A likely consequence of this is that a child's self-esteem may be high at home but lower in the early years setting. Furthermore, if a child moves into a setting in which the adults have expectations of the child based on a lack of understanding about the child's life and experiences outside the setting the child's self-esteem is likely to drop. This lack of understanding can arise due to a lack of knowledge about the child's cultural experiences and assigning a stereotypical identity to the child.

If a child has a high self-esteem he or she is likely to feel that they are significant, that others value them, that they are competent and capable of success, and they are more likely to feel confident about making decisions and meeting new challenges. There is clearly a link between self-esteem and resilience.

## Resilience

Having high self-esteem and a clear sense of their identities is necessary for children to develop resilience. Children who are resilient 'are better equipped to resist stress and adversity, cope with change and uncertainty, and to recover faster and more completely from traumatic events or episodes' (Newman and Blackburn 2002). In everyday terms resilience can be defined as the ability to deal with the highs and lows of life and to adapt to challenging circumstances or situations.

Resilience is an important aspect of emotional development as it encompasses the ability to communicate with others, to be willing to attempt to solve problems, to be able to control and channel negative thoughts and feelings, and to be confident and optimistic that things will work out in the end (Grotberg 1995). Without resilience children may feel powerless, sad, anxious, frightened and unable to rise to new challenges.

Resilience and self-esteem are closely linked in that developing resilience requires, among other things, early attachments, confidence of being valued and loved and a clear sense of self-identity (including a strong cultural identity) (Payne and Butler 2003)

While it is true that some children within our settings will have experienced very traumatic events or episodes (e.g. war, experience of being a refugee, homelessness, death within the family) we also need to recognize that all children face challenges and change within their lives – no child is exempt. Moving home, starting with a new childminder, the birth of a new sibling, making the transition from home to nursery or from nursery to school are the types of challenges and changes all children have to deal with. Fostering resilience in children is an important aspect of their emotional development as it enables them to face change and uncertainty, and to manage negative emotions such as anxiety and insecurity rather than be overwhelmed by them.

## Children's rights

Adopting a children's rights perspective enables us to move away from age- and stage-related goals and to broaden our understanding of what young children need to support their social and emotional development. In the United Nations Convention on the Rights of the Child (UNCRC) children's rights can be sorted into three categories: provision rights, protection rights and participation rights. The UNCRC has been criticized for presenting and maintaining a western understanding of childhood, not least in that it presents the child as a self-contained individual. In many societies and cultures this concept of the child is unknown or unfamiliar.

There is, however, much that is positive in the UNCRC. There is an emphasis, for example, on children's right to express their opinion and have that opinion taken into account in matters affecting the child (UNCRC:

Article 12). The UNCRC provides us with another perspective on children's social and emotional development as it emphasizes the need to listen to children and respond to what the children tell us rather than expecting the children to fit in with the provision we make for them. In listening to children more we may become more aware of what they need to develop their identities, confidence and positive self-esteem.

The UNCRC also stresses that whatever is done must be in the child's best interests. There will always be some debate about what is 'best' for a child. In the New Zealand curriculum guidelines, for example, it is stated of well-being in Strand 1 that: 'All children have a right to health, protection from harm and anxiety, and to harmony, consistency, affection, firmness, warmth, and sensitivity . . . They need as much consistency and continuity of experience as possible in order to develop confidence and trust' (New Zealand Ministry of Education 1996: 46).

You may agree and feel that children should be protected from harm and anxiety, but a certain amount of anxiety is part of life. So, do you think we should be protecting children from anxiety or enabling children to cope with anxiety and in so doing helping them develop their resilience? Dealing with transition, for example, is a part of everyone's life and transitions may be the cause of much anxiety. It is wiser, therefore, to concentrate on supporting young children through transitions and in so doing help to develop their resilience rather than thinking about ways of avoiding transitions.

## Transitions and children's emotional development

Transition can be understood in terms of 'the influence of contexts (for example, family, classroom, community) and the connections among these contexts (e.g. family–school relationships) at any given time and across time' (Pianta *et al.* 1999: 4, cited in Dockett and Perry 2001). If we are concerned about the development of children's confidence, self-identity and self-esteem we need to consider how best to support children during various transitions.

Babies and children experience a wide range of changes and transitions in which they move from the familiar (e.g. their home environment) to the unfamiliar (e.g. their early years setting or school). It is important not to underestimate the range, number and impact of transitions that very young children may experience. A study examining stress levels of toddlers making the transition from home to childcare found that their stress levels were high as much as five months after first attending a childcare setting (Ahnert *et al.* 2004). The study highlights the need to think carefully about how to provide ongoing support for very young children within the childcare setting, and how to manage the transition process sensitively.

If the transition is to be a positive experience it is important to manage it sensitively and with an awareness of the complexity of what transition involves. Transitions are not always smooth for all children. This is acknowledged in various guidance and policy documents, particularly with respect to transitions to school and from one key stage to another (e.g. DfES 2003a, 2003b; ACCAC 2004)

Children's experiences of transition are unlikely to be identical. The transitions will depend upon factors such as the children's ages and their family circumstances. Furthermore, although children will share some of transitions (e.g. the transition from their home setting to your setting/school) each child's experiences of these transitions are unique.

When considering how to support children through transitions it is important to be aware of how each transition may make different demands on the child. In moving from the home environment to a nursery setting a child moves into a new cultural setting. This involves the child in having to learn new rules (many of which are unspoken and therefore implicit). Children also have to learn new routines and also adopt new roles or identities: they move from being the 'baby' at home to the 'child' in the nursery or the 'pupil' at school.

In one study, approximately half of the Foundation Stage teachers involved felt that certain groups of children found the transition to school difficult. The groups included children with SENs, children who were born in the summer, children without a nursery experience and children without a friendship group at the school (Sanders *et al.* 2005). Earlier research has highlighted how ethnicity may also shape a child's experience of transition to school (Gillborn and Mirza 2000; Sammons *et al.* 2002; DfES 2003a). Early years settings and schools need to look very carefully at how the transition to school may impact on different groups of children, and develop strategies to support children during the transition process. This may entail having to critically reflect on the extent to which the ethos, curriculum and organization within the setting meet children's needs and provide for their interests rather than merely developing strategies to help children 'fit in' to the existing provision.

Strategies aimed at supporting children during transitions need to acknowledge the emotional impact of transitions. Many settings aim to minimize anxieties by encouraging children to visit before they start so that the environment is not completely strange; other produce photo books for children new to the setting to familiarize them with the environment, routines and types of activities (LTS 2007).

Dowling (2000) has emphasized the need for practitioners to be proactive in supporting children during periods of transition rather than waiting until children show obvious signs of distress. Some children communicate their feelings of distress or anxiety by crying or refusing to leave an adult's side, or they may have difficulty concentrating or may appear unable to do things that they were previously able to do. A child's body language provides useful signals of unhappiness or cautiousness.

Research seems to point to the importance of friendships (Dockett and Perry 2001, 2002; Sanders *et al.* 2005) in easing children's transitions. Parents, like their children, feel that friendship groups help children to settle in to new environments. One parent described her small daughter's friends as operating as a 'little support network' (Sanders *et al.* 2005: 59). This aspect of children's social and emotional life is sometimes overlooked by adults, who may feel that making new friends is more important than maintaining existing friendships, but a sizeable proportion of settings seem to have recognized the emotionally supportive role that peers and friends can play during transition and have set up various 'buddy' systems (Ofsted 2007).

Babies and young children may experience numerous transitions within an early years setting, including adapting to staff absences, changeover of staff due to shift systems and holidays, moving to different rooms for naps or meals, experiencing going to sleep with one member of staff present and waking with another. Research suggests that babies and young children need responsive adults to provide a secure base (Murray and Trevarthen 1992; Miller *et al.* 1993, cited in Elfer 2004). Both the *Birth to Three Matters Framework* (Sure Start 2002) and *Birth to Three: Supporting Our Youngest Children* (LTS 2005) emphasize how important a relationship with a key person in the setting is in terms of children's emotional security and development. In an ideal world, the key person provides the secure base babies and young children need and is also able to 'tune in' to the child and help her negotiate some of the transitions and new experiences she encounters. In the real world, often for organizational reasons, the key person may not always be available and settings therefore may need to take a critical look at how young children are provided with the emotional support they need. We should also be asking ourselves whether the emphasis on the need for one key person reflects an uncritical acceptance of the dominant childcare discourse. Are there other ways in which settings can provide a secure emotional base for young children?

## Supporting children: some practical strategies for supporting children's personal, social and emotional development

Dowling (2000) has argued that emotional health depends upon children being able to experience and express a range of emotions. Young children need to talk about both positive and negative emotions. Central government has shown an increasing interest in the issue of children's personal, social and emotional health and development. In *Promoting Children's Mental Health within Early Years Settings* (DfES 2001) mentally healthy children are described as those who are able to:

1. Develop psychologically, emotionally, intellectually and spiritually
2. Initiate, develop and sustain mutually satisfying personal relationships
3. Use and enjoy solitude
4. Become aware of others and empathise with them
5. Play and learn
6. Develop a sense of right and wrong
7. Resolve (face) problems and setbacks and learn from them.

(DfES 2001: 6)

Bearing in mind the cultural diversity within this country it is important to reflect on whether these indicators are sufficiently broad to be able to accommodate children's differing patterns of social and emotional development.

In 2005 the DfES published a set of resources known as SEAL (Social and Emotional Aspects of Learning). These curriculum resources were designed explicitly to promote social, emotional and behavioural skills and it is particularly significant that these materials aimed to help children become aware of and able to express and describe their emotions. The materials have been influenced by the work of Howard Gardner and Daniel Goleman and the concept of emotional literacy.

In the early 1990s Howard Gardner's work on multiple intelligences received attention. Two of the multiple intelligences Gardner identified were intra-personal intelligence and inter-personal intelligence (Gardner 1993). Intra-personal intelligence concerns knowing about one's own feelings, while inter-personal intelligence is the ability to identify and understand the feelings of others. Daniel Goleman further developed the concept of emotional intelligence and identified five aspects of emotional intelligence: self awareness (recognizing your feelings), emotional control, self-motivation, empathy and handling relationships.

Some children will communicate how they are feeling through forms of behaviour that may be described as unacceptable or 'challenging'. One approach to this issue has been to locate 'problem' behaviour or 'emotional problems' within individual children and develop strategies for helping the individual children concerned exhibit more pro-social behaviours. An alternative approach is based on the premise that the identities, skills and behaviours an individual develops are related to the social contexts they experience. Linke (1998) has argued that children's own behaviour and attitudes towards others will be influenced by the cultures in which they grow up. Children growing up in cultures valuing competition and self-reliance are likely to react to and treat others differently to those children who are brought up in cultures valuing community and inter-personal support. Maybin and Woodhead (2003) have drawn on research in Canada and the USA to show how children are encouraged to express their emotions and relate to others. In South Baltimore, white, working-class mothers teach their young daughters to 'stand up for themselves' by encouraging them to react aggressively in response to their mothers' teasing (Miller and Sperry 1987, cited in Maybin and Woodhead 2003). In contrast, through the nature of adults' interactions with them, children in the Inuit Utkuhiksalingmiut community are taught that expressions of anger, hostility, bad temper and greed are disapproved of (Briggs 1970, 1998, cited in Maybin and Woodhead 2003).

If a child communicates their unhappiness through 'challenging' behaviour it is not enough to try to change the individual child. Instead we need to be looking at what experiences the child has and the discourses she or he has access to. This means that practitioners need to reflect on the ethos of their setting and the messages, both overt and covert, that children are getting about how people are genuinely valued. If the early years setting or school does not have an ethos that emphasizes caring, respect, honesty, a sense of community, and so on, then attempts at, for example, helping a child feel more confident or raising children's self-esteem are likely to founder. It would be unrealistic to suggest that there will never be some children who, for a range of frequently complex reasons, will require more individualized support. However, the more effective the provision is in supporting children's personal, social and emotional development the fewer the number of children that will require individual intervention (DfES 2005).

## Conclusion

This chapter has looked at how considering young children's social and emotional development involves more than enabling children to meet predetermined goals or markers. We need to think about how to help children gain a sense of who they are and negotiate their way through the range of discourses to which they have access, develop their resilience and foster their self-esteem.

## Points for reflection

- In your setting, what seems to be regarded as a 'normal' pattern of emotional development? To what extent is this culturally specific?
- How do your transition practices help to build children's resilience?
- How are parents able to share with you their ideas about child rearing and their views about how best to support young children's emotional development?
- Does the ethos within your setting help build children's self- esteem? How do you know?
- What strategies would you like to introduce or develop to enable young children to express and communicate their feelings?

## References

ACCAC (Qualifications, Curriculum and Assessment Authority for Wales) (2004) *The Foundation Phase in Wales: A Draft Framework for Children's Learning*. Cardiff: ACCAC.

Ahnert, L., Gunnar, M.R., Lamb, M.E. and Barthel, M. (2004) Transition to child care: association with infant-mother attachment, infant negative emotion and cortisol elevations, *Child Development*, 75(3).

Archard, R. (1993) *Children's Rights and Childhood*. London: Routledge.

Browne, N. (2004) *Gender Equity in the Early Years*. Maidenhead: Open University Press.

Commons, M.L. and Miller, P.M. (1998) Emotional learning in infants: a cross-cultural examination. Paper presented at the American Association for the Advancement of Science Philadelphia, PA, February.

Department for Education and Skills (DfES) (2001) *Guidance Document: Promoting Children's Mental Health within Early Years Settings*. Nottingham: DfES.

Department for Education and Skills (DfES) (2003a) *Aiming High: Raising the Achievement of Minority Ethnic Pupils*. Nottingham: DfES.

Department for Education and Skills (DfES) (2003b) *Excellence and Enjoyment: A Strategy for Primary Schools*. Nottingham: (DfES).

Department for Education and Skills (DfES) (2005) *Excellence and Enjoyment: Social and Emotional Aspects of Learning (SEAL)*, http://publications.teachernet.gov.uk/ (accessed 30 April 2007).

Department for Education and Skills (DfES) (2006) *The Early Years Foundation Stage – Consultation on a Single Quality Framework for Services to Children from Birth to Five*, DfES, http://www.dfes.gov.uk/consultations/conResults.cfm?consultationId=1393 (accessed 7 March 2007).

Dockett, S., and Perry, B., (2001) Starting school: effective transitions, *Early Childhood Research and Practice*, 3(2) Fall, http://ecrp.uiuc.edu/v3n2/dockett.html (accessed 7 March 2007).

Dockett, S. and Perry, B. (2002) Who's ready for what? Young children starting school, *Contemporary Issues in Early Childhood*, 3(1): 67–89.

Donaldson, M. (1978) *Children's Minds*. London: Fontana.

Dowling, M. (2000) *Young Children's Personal, Social and Emotional Development*. London: Paul Chapman.

Elfer, P. (2004) Building intimacy in relationships with young children, in L. Miller and J. Devereux (eds) *Supporting Children's Learning in the Early Years*. London: David Fulton.

Farver, J.A. and Shin, Y.L. (1997) Social pretend play in Korean and Anglo-American pre-schoolers, *Child Development*, 68(3): 544–557.

Gardner, H. (1993) *Multiple Intelligences*. New York: Basic Books.

Gillborn, D. and Mirza, H.S. (2000) *Educational Inequality: Mapping Race, Class and Gender. A Synthesis of Research Evidence*. London: Ofsted.

Grotberg, E. (1995) *A Guide to Promoting Resilience in Children: Strengthening the Human Spirit, Practice and Reflections 8*. The Hague: Bernard Van Leer Foundation.

Hughes, M. (1986) *Children and Number: Difficulties in Learning Mathematics*. Oxford: Blackwell.

Learning and Teaching Scotland (LTS) (2005) *Birth to Three: Supporting Our Youngest Children*. Edinburgh: Scottish Executive.

Learning and Teaching Scotland (LTS) Early Years (2007) *Sharing Practice: Emotional, Personal and Social Development*,http://www.ltscotland.org.uk/earlyyears/sharingpractice/keyaspects/emotionalpersonalsocial/index.asp (accessed 6 March 2007).

LeVine, R.A., Dixon, S., LeVine, S., Richman, A., Leiderman, P.H., Keefer, C.H. and Brazelton, T.B. (1994) *Childcare and Culture: Lessons from Africa*. New York: Cambridge University Press.

Linke, P. (1998) *Let's Stop Bullying*. Watson, ACT: Australian Early Childhood Association.

Maybin, J. and Woodhead, M. (eds) (2003) *Childhood, U212*. Milton Keynes: Open University.

Murray, L. and Trevarthen, C. (1992) 'Emotional regulation of interactions between two month olds and their mothers' in A. Alverez (ed) *Live Company Psychoanalytical Psychotherapy with Autistic, Borderline, Deprived and Abused Children*, London: Routledge.

New Zealand Ministry of Education (1996), *Te Whàriki, Early Childhood Curriculum*. Wellington, New Zealand: Ministry of Education.

Newman, T. and Blackburn, S. (Barnardo's Policy, Research and Influencing Unit) (2002) *Interchange 78: Transitions in the Lives of Children and Young People: Resilience Factors*. Edinburgh: The Scottish Executive Education

Department.

Ofsted (2007) *The Foundation Stage: A Survey of 144 Settings*. London: HMI.

Payne, H. and Butler, I. ( 2003) *Quality Protects Research Briefing – No 9: Promoting the Mental Health of Children in Need*. Nottingham: DfES, Research in Practice.

Penn, H. (2005) *Understanding Childhood: Issues and Controversies*. Maidenhead: Open University Press.

Qualifications and Curriculum Authority (QCA)/Department for Education and Employment (DfEE) (2000) *Curriculum Guidance for the Foundation Stage*. London: QCA/DfEE.

Sammons, P., Sylva, K., Melhuish, E.C., Siraj-Blatchford, I., Taggart, B. and Elliot, K. (2002) Measuring the impact of pre-school on children's cognitive progress over the pre-school period, *EPPE Technical Paper 8a*. London: Institute of Education.

Sanders, D., White, G., Burge, B., Sharp, C., Eames, A., McEune, R. and Grayson, H. (2005) *A Study of the Transition from the Foundation Stage to Key Stage 1* (DfES Research Report SSU/2005/FR/013). London: Sure Start/ NFER.

Sure Start (2002) *Birth to Three Matters Framework*. London: Sure Start.

UN (1989) *United Nations Convention on the Rights of the Child, Children's Rights Network*, http://www.crin.org/docs/resources/treaties/uncrc.htm (accessed 12 June 2005).

# 5 What's your attitude? Inclusion and early years settings

## Jonathan Rix

## Where do you start?

Early September, and a new intake of children arrives in your setting: twenty to thirty new characters to fill your working days. Who are they? How do you identify them? What behaviours grab your attention? What sorts of knowledge interest you? What appearances affect you? Do you quite quickly (consciously or subconsciously) categorize these children, putting an informal (or formal) label on them: the 'quiet one', the 'ball of energy', the one who's 'going to be a handful' ... ?

All of us group and label others. As Foucault (1978) makes clear, we have to position ourselves within the dominant structure of the normalizing society. We constitute our own identities, and identify other's identities, in the context of social relationships and structures. A key factor in defining ourselves and others is positioning ourselves within social categories. We respond to others and their behaviours on the basis of whether we perceive them to be insiders or outsiders of the category in which we place ourselves (Waterhouse 2004). This means that the same behaviour produces a different response in us dependent on how we perceive the individual.

Take my son. He used to touch people's bottoms and other private bits in public places. When he did, the person would spin around ready to demand an apology ... and suddenly look all forgiving and laugh. My son wasn't what they were expecting. He's a very pretty red-headed boy with Down syndrome. 'Ohhh', they'd go, 'bless ... ' or something similar. His perceived difference meant he could get away with loads of stuff no one else his age could. So what's wrong with that? Isn't that a perk of having an extra chromosome 21 in your cells? Or is it a way to teach this child to be different? To behave in a way that only those who are different would behave? Is it a way to create behaviours that others can later identify and use to justify exclusionary actions?

How you perceive and respond to children has an ongoing impact that begins with you and them, but can lead in all kinds of directions. For example, when a teacher chooses to take a close working interest in a child with Down syndrome then other children are more likely to engage with them too (Fox *et al*. 2004). It has both an academic and social pay-off. Similar effects can be seen for a whole range of children. If a teacher sees a child as their responsibility then it brings great benefits in their communication and interaction with that person (Rix and Hall 2006). Put simply, inclusion begins with *your* attitude.

## Starting with your self

The key aim of reflexivity is developing a deeper understanding of your own views and ways of working and behaving, the context in which you are operating, and the perspective of others. This involves reflecting on the techniques and concepts you are applying to a situation and the cultural and moral assumptions that underpin their application. You are developing a perspective that allows you 'to produce new actions that improve the situation or trigger a reframing of the problem' (Schön 1983: 277). You cannot understand everything, but you *can* identify possible routes to better practice, possible barriers to engagement and possible means to overcome them . . . as well as strengths to build upon!

A good place to start is to consider your views about disability, ethnicity, class, gender, faith groups, sexual orientation and what constitutes appropriate social behaviours. Even if you feel that you are utterly fair-minded and treat all equally you are probably responding differently without being aware of it. The weight of research, both observational and statistical, shows how heavily biased our systems are against certain individuals across different contexts . . . and the system is made up of people who generally want to be utterly fair-minded and treat all equally.

Look at the picture in Figure 5.1. What is the first thought that comes into your mind?

Is it two children in wheelchairs, or two children playing catch? To their friends the first thing would be their names; to a medical practitioner it may be why the children need to be in wheelchairs; to a bus driver it may be that she has to get the ramp out . . . What would your first thoughts be if these children arrived on that September morning? Would you immediately start to worry about practical problems? Would you immediately start thinking about opportunities for learning? Or would you want to get to know the children first?

Such reflection can occur both in the moment and over longer periods of time. It can be both an internal, self-analytic act and an external one, involving discussion with others. It is both personal and communal.

**Figure 5.1:** What do you see?

## Thinking about a problem of inclusion

When you are 'reframing a problem', do you start by considering why you might feel it is a problem? Is considering it to be a problem the main barrier? Staff at my son's local primary school took about six months to recognize and talk about strategies as 'opportunities for others' rather than as solutions to 'his problems'.

Do you consider if the problem is situated within an individual or within the context of the situation in which the individuals co-exist? Do you start with the child's difference or with your response to each child and the manner in which the context is supportive of that child? Many children – even at a very young age – are already used to being excluded by social systems:

> When I first went to the nursery I didn't like it and I used to try and run out of the door with my Dad. I didn't know what the food was' (Vlora, an Albanian girl aged 6, quoted in Rutter 2001: 169).

By questioning the immediate and wider social context, you are better placed to consider whether their behaviour is a result of previous exclusion and/or resistance to further exclusion. Even very young children may have been marginalized by a traumatic personal experience, or excluded by more everyday responses from people to such things as their size or looks or behaviours. Your response can easily reinforce this exclusion or challenge it.

When you wish to explore the impact of your power within a relationship you could identify your role, identity and viewpoint within that context –

your subject positions. This requires considering the external experiences and influences that shape and inhabit an individual's understanding of their situation and the wider context. Drawing upon Heron's (2005) work, you could consider the following questions.

- What power relations operate here?
- What subject positions do I and this other individual occupy?
- How are we 'empowered' and 'disempowered' in this relationship?
- What and how are we resisting – personally and within a wider context?
- What value and effort do I invest in understanding how to provide equal service to all? Why this level?
- How does this investment act as a barrier or facilitator for others?
- What self-image do I have as a result of my good intentions towards different social/ethnic/cultural/gender groups?
- What happens to my self-image if I see myself as having failed in respect to my good intentions?
- Have I failed? Have I, in fact, been unequal in my work with these individuals?

The purpose of asking such questions is not to make you feel guilty. They are a means of examining and challenging your unspoken biases and those that exist within the systems around you, and of identifying factors from which you and others can learn.

Consider the actions of this reception class teacher, Susie, when her teaching assistant, Anna, takes control of a boy, Jared, in her class. Jared is a child with autism:

> Jared joins Susie at the literacy table but once again argues with her about her instructions, saying that she can't tell him to sit and that he won't if she asks. He leaves the table but Anna gets him back. It is clear that Susie now feels awkward and undermined. Susie controls her own sense of frustration, but tells off another distracted boy with more firmness than she might typically. (Rix 2004)

In this context Susie finds her typical power relations being usurped. She's the least powerful in this context. She's wishing to support her empowered teaching assistant. She's also aware that Jared is not at ease with a number of assumed social practices. It's important to her to be even-handed in her exchanges and so she allows herself to be potentially diminished in the eyes of those around her. Yet this leaves her feeling vulnerable. The effort that this entails results in her reassertion of power over another individual. Importantly, though, at the time of making these observations, Susie was unaware that she had told off the other boy. Her reassertion of power was not a conscious decision. She was more aware of the impact of her behaviours with the labelled child and her colleague than with other pupils in her class.

Perhaps this last point would be the most important lesson of all for Susie in this exchange? The challenge for all practitioners is that inclusion is about everyone in the setting, not just a selected few. We have to examine our behaviours and values and their impact in the moment as an ongoing part of our working lives.

## Starting with the children

It is not just your assumptions that need consideration; children's behaviours and communications are affected by a range of possible physical, emotional, personal, social, cultural, intellectual and situational factors (Figure 5.2). These contextual factors frame the ways in which messages and meanings are expressed and interpreted. In some situations these factors can interfere with our ability to communicate (such as in the example of Susie above), and at other times they can ease the process of communication. This in turn affects the context for further messages.

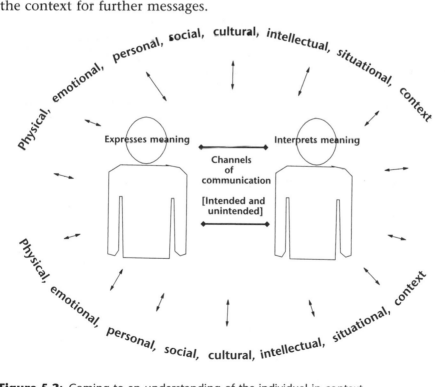

**Figure 5.2:** Coming to an understanding of the individual in context

## The importance of listening

A central aspect of both inclusive and reflective practice is listening. Active listening is a particularly effective way for both adults and children to gain understanding of another person's ideas. It encourages the speaker to engage more fully in the communication. It requires that *you* show that *you* are listening. It is not simply responsive, it is about engaging with the views of the individual, and taking the time to explore the meaning and the impact of that meaning. Listening is not just an aural activity, either. It can be seen as a holistic process, involving all our faculties to interpret the experiences being evidenced by others:

> Listening to the hundred, the thousand languages, symbols and codes we use to express ourselves and communicate, and with which life expresses itself and communicates to those who know how to listen (Rinaldi 2005: 20).

Rinaldi recognizes listening as more than actively engaging with what is being said. It involves sensitivity to the ways we connect with others, using all our senses to access the languages, symbols and codes used to communicate and to express ourselves. You must listen to yourself as well. This listening responds to influence by emotion. It requires us to be open to change, to be questioning and doubting of certainties, suspending judgements and prejudices. As a consequence, those involved in the communication become visible, they are recognized and can see themselves recognized. Legitimized in presenting and re-evaluating ideas, processes and beliefs, they are provided with the basis for a learning relationship.

## Seeing the child as active and knowledgeable

Children are neither static entities nor passive ones:

> Disabled children, like other children and adults, are flexible social beings whose behavioural patterns, communication abilities, level of involvement and level of interest will vary over the duration of an activity (Davis and Watson 2000: 213).

They bring with them understandings, skills and experiences. This social and cultural capital (Bourdieu 1983) underlies the child's engagement with the social and cultural situations he or she faces. Consider the following example. Nazma is three and a half, and her home language is Pahari. Her mother believes that school is the place to learn English:

Nazma's nursery teacher reported that she was very upset during her first weeks in nursery. Her teacher also commented on Nazma's self-sufficient and stubborn personality ... Her nursery teacher commented ... that Nazma 'came to life' with the bilingual classroom assistant and viewed mother tongue support as crucially important for her personal, social, emotional and language development. (Parke and Drury 2001: 124)

Imagine the problems facing Nazma if her teacher didn't appreciate the importance of her home language. Imagine the route her active self would have taken her down. Her 'stubborn personality' could become problematized, marginalized and demotivated, and speaking English would be seen as an even greater source of conflict.

## Avoiding assumptions, challenging fixed positions

How do you come to know the children you work with? Do you discuss them with their parents, with your colleagues, with outside practitioners, with the children themselves? Do you carry out detailed normative assessment or do you engage with children in the activity and explore their progress through formative assessment? Do you let them define their interests in a curricular context or do you impose what children do throughout their day? Do you seek out their views or rely upon your own experiences? It is not uncommon for practitioners to do the latter. For example, the rare questions teachers do ask about prior knowledge focus upon what has been taught in earlier lessons (Myhill and Brackley 2004). This reinforces the notion that the knowledge children bring from outside the setting is less important than academic, taught knowledge. It also means that numerous learning opportunities are being missed. And how can the effectiveness of any teaching strategy be assessed if a measurement of knowledge at the end does not accurately include the prior level of knowledge?

If we do not ask questions we must make assumptions about what children know. The chances are high that we'll make mistakes. My son, Robbie, for example, went to both a special school nursery and a local playgroup. At the nursery they set a learning target of 'drinking from an open beaker', even though he was already doing this at the local playgroup – because that was the sort of cup everyone used.

Overestimating children's knowledge is as much a problem as underestimating it. It creates gaps in the learning environment that children may fill with confusion, lack of interest and/or behaviours that the practitioner may regard as inappropriate. Parke *et al.* (2002) describe gaps opening up as a result of a discordance between knowledge of home and school language and the lack of bilingual opportunities in early years settings. For example, Samia is a 4-year-old bilingual girl, seen as 'silent' in her nursery class, who is a competent codeswitcher between Pahari and classroom English when playing 'school' with her brother at home; and six 7 year olds are seen as noisy and disruptive in assemblies, which often have solely second-language religious content, but listen attentively when the Qur'an is being read in their first and second language.

These examples also underline the exclusionary risk of thinking that what you see is all there is, or from judging linguistic and intellectual development of children from a solitary perspective. This risk is exacerbated when practitioners use this partial insight to judge an individual against a particular timetable of development, such as the levels of the National Curriculum, or particular stages in language acquisition, and plan on the basis of these. In some of these examples, too, practitioners had to be aware of children's underutilized skills, but could not, or would not, take advantage of them. Why is it that practitioners should choose to not build upon skills that are in evidence or resist drawing upon information they are receiving from a child? After all, ignoring what you know about children's knowledge is bound to create an exclusionary risk, opening up those gaps with the potential to be filled with lack of interest, frustration or unwanted behaviours.

Consider this example from a playgroup, in which signals from the child are being ignored. The practitioner has already tried four times to get Josh to write his name.

> The children are then given shapes worksheets and Josh says, 'Go away I don't want a pencil' he pushes away the pencil and paper. He says, 'I don't need mine anymore he can have it' (referring to a child who is unwell and is lying on the cushions in the book area). Josh tries to leave the table but the adult persuades him to stay and colour in a blue circle. He colours it in very quickly. She asks him to do a 'J' for his name but he says he can't do it. She says next time she will do dots for him so he can do a 'J'. He says, 'Yes dots'. He goes off to lie on the floor saying, 'I'm tired'. (Miller and Paige-Smith 2004: 131)

In this example the practitioners introduced a formal literacy activity because they felt under pressure from the curriculum and parents to do so, and in the hope that it would prepare the children for primary school. The practitioner was not really reacting to the child but was instead trying to get him to achieve in the context of parameters constructed elsewhere, including within her own set of values. She cannot let go of the activity, nor can she allow the child to let go of it. As a consequence she has to face behaviours that are neither conducive to learning nor to a fulfilling working day. It is not difficult to see both the practitioner and the child as excluded through this process.

## Starting with your practice

In reading this chapter you may feel there have been a number of contradictions. Here are some examples:

- encouraging you to not use labels and yet using them myself
- describing a problem as a state of mind, while framing this as a problem
- encouraging you to suspend judgements and prejudices, yet asking you to explore them
- suggesting that children are enabled both through having choice (e.g. Nazma) and through having no choice (e.g. Robbie)
- asking you to trust your feelings but question them
- describing exclusion as being a moment in which both the practitioner and the child are excluded.

One of the challenges and pleasures of inclusion is that it is full of such possible contradictions. It is about tensions and rough edges. One of the most challenging is the need to respect and build upon a child's views and prior knowledge, yet at the same time confronting the biases that exist within them. Children from a very early age have many biases well established. Research in Australia (Davies 1991, 1993), for example, demonstrated that within early years settings young people commonly respond to stories in a stereotypical, gendered manner, even if the stories remove stereotypical roles. Of course, much in our society and culture encourages negative stereotypes. For example, evil or tragic characters in classic children's books often have some sort of physical impairment (e.g. Long John Silver and Tiny Tim). If you wish children to move beyond these hidden (or not so hidden) biases then you have to encourage them to take a critical perspective on experiences. It may feel as if throughout this process you risk setting your values (and the education system's values?) against those of the child and the culture from which they come, creating the opportunity for exclusion. The lesson of inclusion, however, is that through encouraging children to engage in other people's perspectives, particularly through peer group interactive approaches, opportunities can be created to explore and reflect on such issues. Through this process children can come to see that possible contradictions are only contradictions if you see them from one fixed, unquestioning perspective.

## Viewing it from another perspective

Another concern I have about this chapter is that it may have a negative tone. By encouraging you to question your attitudes and practices, it may feel as if it's suggesting there is something fundamentally wrong about them. This is not my intention. I hope that the reflective process helps you find much that is positive and provides you with inclusive opportunities. Susan Hart (1996) described how much that can enhance learning is overlooked because people are searching for the things that get in the way of the learning, or for things that they believe can be improved. She considers experiences and actions not because they are a source of difficulties but because they are a 'source of insight into possibilities'. She named this reflexive process 'innovative thinking'.

Hart recognized that to better understand the learning situation she needed to consider as many perspectives as possible. When working with children she recommended the following approaches.

- *Making connections:* attempt to understand how the child's response is affected by their environment and experience, and in what ways these can be influenced by the practitioner.
- *Contradicting:* attempt to create a legitimate contradictory reading of the child's response, revealing the underlying assumptions that make us see a child's response as problematic.
- *The child's eye view:* attempt to see in what way the child's response is active and logical from their perspective.
- *The impact of feelings:* attempt to understand in what way our interpretation of the child's response is a consequence of projecting our own hopes and fears.
- *Suspending judgement:* attempt to stand back from the analysis, and question to what degree the information you have is enough for the actions you are taking.

A key component of this innovative thinking approach is that it includes the context. The child is not the only focus. You move beyond your traditional response to explore other possibilities. Such an approach has value beyond the student/practitioner relationship, when considering issues related to anyone from a parent to a colleague to yourself!

Consider the following experience that I went through with my son when carrying out early intervention activities. I was a parent in a teaching role and I used an innovative thinking approach, across a period of weeks, to explore what might be happening and how to make the experience inclusive for us both.

I am happily doing early intervention activities at the table with Robbie, such as picture-matching games and 'where are the three little pigs hiding?' As usual, though, when I get out the sound cards he knocks them from the table and tries to get down from his seat.

I considered the formality of the table as a problem, and the length of time he sat there. I wondered if I gave some sort of cue of uncertainty before starting the cards ... a sort of 'oh no, here we go again' signal. Maybe Robbie understood that he couldn't do these sounds yet, and didn't wish to waste his time. Maybe he found them boring. Maybe the clear focus on his communication difficulties was too threatening to him. Maybe he enjoyed picking cards up off the floor. Maybe he was saying he wanted to do the activity somewhere else. Maybe he recognized that his friends and siblings never have to do this type of activity and so didn't see why he had to. Maybe he was annoyed that I had not listened to his previous complaints about doing this activity or doing it in this way. Maybe I felt under too much pressure to make him use these sound cards because I believed the professionals who told me that this is one of the best tools for developing sound production. Could I be absolutely sure that developing speech was his most important communication priority? Maybe developing his signing skills would be of greater immediate value to him. Was this a skill I could contribute to?

Asking the questions did not of itself produce an answer, but it provided a variety of options for changing practice that meant I arrived at a solution that included us both. As a result of all these questions, I changed where I did the activity, how I did it, when I did it and with whom I did it. For example, I did it on the floor, on the stairs, all around the kitchen, with his mother, sister and next-door neighbour, going upstairs to play, after lunch at his grandparents, and while swinging on the swing. Then I gave it up for a while ... then tried again ... And in the end I decided to do only those activities he selected. As a result he did not choose to engage with sound cards again until he started using Jolly Phonics with the rest of his reception class.

## Opening up to others

At the heart of inclusive practice is the collaboration that creates learning opportunities for both adult and child. Just as we support children within the setting, so too do we need to support and be supported by all those with whom we work and the systems we create. Research repeatedly shows that practitioners who are involved in good teamwork are more effective, enthusiastic and confident about inclusion. Consider these comments by Lara, who taught pupils with English as an additional language at Cleves Primary School:

> Everyone is valued here ... they are encouraged to use English and their first language as well ... it is the ethos of the whole school, not just a few

individual teachers ... Here, it is about equality, no matter who you are, what you look like, what you do, we are all the same, we all have something to contribute. (Alderson 1999: 40)

This collaborative and cooperative perspective encourages a broader reflexivity, so you are less likely to make unquestioned assumptions. It encourages you to draw on a wider range of resources within the immediate learning situation and beyond, providing you with more opportunities to plan for learning, and helping you to be more flexible in your moment-by-moment interactions. It encourages, too, an ethos in which individual children can more readily support each other's learning, where they become responsible for one another, and come to recognize the value of a whole range of skills that are not easily prescribed within a formal curriculum. The consequence of such peer interaction is not just a positive academic outcome but a social one too (Nind *et al.* 2004).

## Conclusion: recognizing we are doing this together

Inclusion begins with an attitude. It only works if you believe it is your responsibility to make it work. Inclusion encourages you to reflect on your views about group identities, behaviours and roles, and your responses to them. It asks you to consider the manner in which you invest your own identity within such group identities, behaviours and roles. In approaching children with whom you work, you can try to view them in the context of their lives, listening to them, recognizing their knowledge and trying to avoid imposing your assumptions upon them. You can see the challenges you are presented with as opportunities. In so doing you try to shift perspectives, to engage with the views of others, and encourage them in turn to engage more widely. The great thing about children, however, is that they require very little encouragement to do all of this for themselves, and so in the process you too may learn far more than you ever expected.

## Points for reflection

- Do you see it as your responsibility to work with all children? If not, how could you?
- Do you consider the impact of your own values on the judgements you make? If not, how could you?
- Do you come to understand people in the context of their life beyond the setting? If not, how could you?

- Do you question the impact of the teaching and learning practices and context on the engagement of children? If not, how could you?
- Do you value the learning strengths and current knowledge of children when developing activities? If not, how could you?
- Do you always encourage peers to support each other's learning? If not, how could you?
- Do you collaborate with your colleagues and the wider community? If not, how could you?
- Do you regard each other as a learning resource? If not, why not give it a go?

## Further reading

Mollard, C. (2003) *Why It's Worth It: Inclusive Education: A Parent's Perspective*. Edinburgh: SHS Trust.
Parents for Inclusion (n.d.) http://www.parentsforinclusion.org/.
Whalley, M. (2001) *Involving Parents in their Children's Learning*. London: Paul Chapman.

## References

Alderson, P. (ed.) (1999) *Learning and Inclusion: The Cleves School Experience*. London: David Fulton.
Bourdieu, P. (1983) Economic capital, cultural capital, social capital. Soziale-Welt, Supplement 2: 183–198.
Davies, B. (1991) *Frogs and Snails and Feminist Tales: Preschool Children and Gender*. North Sydney, Australia: Allen & Unwin.
Davies, B. (1993) *Shards of Glass: Children Reading and Writing Beyond Gendered Identities*, Cresskill, NJ: Hampton Press.
Davis, J. and Watson, N. (2000) Disabled children's rights in everyday life: problematising notions of competency and promoting self-empowerment, *International Journal of Children's Rights*, 8: 211–228.
Foucault, M. (1978) *The History of Sexuality*, Vol. I. New York: Pantheon.
Fox, S., Farell, P. and Davis, P. (2004) Factors associated with the effective inclusion of primary-aged pupils with Down syndrome, *British Journal of Special Education*, 31(4): 184–190.
Hart, S. (1996) *Beyond Special Needs: Enhancing Children's Learning through Innovative Thinking*. London: Paul Chapman.
Heron, B. (2005) Self-reflection in critical social work practice: subjectivity and the possibilities of resistance, *Reflective Practice*, 6(3): 341–351.

Miller, L. and Paige-Smith, A. (2004) Practitioners' beliefs and children's experiences of literacy in four early years settings, *Early Years*, 24(2): 121–133.

Myhill, D. and Brackley, M. (2004) Making connections: teachers' use of children's prior knowledge in whole class discourse, *British Journal of Educational Studies*, 52(3): 263–275.

Nind, M. and Wearmouth, J. with Collins, J., Hall, K., Rix, J. and Sheehy, K. (2004) A systematic review of pedagogical approaches that can effectively include children with special educational needs in mainstream classrooms with a particular focus on peer group interactive approaches, in *Research Evidence in Education Library*. London: EPPI-Centre, Social Science Research Unit, Institute of Education, University of London.

Parke, T. and Drury, R. (2001) Language development at home and school: gains and losses in young bilinguals, *Early Years, Journal of International Research and Development*, 21(2): 117–128.

Parke, T., Drury, R., Kenner, C. and Helavaara Robertson, L. (2002) Revealing invisible worlds: connecting the mainstream with bilingual children's home and community learning, *Journal of Early Childhood Literacy*, 2(2):195–220.

Rinaldi, C. (2005) Documentation and assessment: what is the relationship? in A. Clark, A. Kjørholt and P. Moss (eds) *Beyond Listening: Children's Perspectives on Early Childhood Services*. Bristol: The Policy Press.

Rix, J. and Hall, K. with Nind, M., Sheehy, K. and Wearmouth, J. (2006) A systematic review of interactions in pedagogical approaches with reported outcomes for the academic and social inclusion of pupils with special educational needs. Technical report, in *Research Evidence in Education Library*. London: EPPI-Centre, Social Science Research Unit, Institute of Education, University of London.

Rix, J. with Tan, A. and Moden, S. (2004) A balance of power: observing a teaching assistant, in R. Hancock and J. Collins (eds) *Primary Teaching Assistants: Learners and Learning*. London: David Fulton: 193–199.

Rutter, J. (2001) *Supporting Refugee Children in Twentieth Century Britain*. Stoke-on-Trent: Trentham Books.

Schön, D. (1983) *The Reflective Practitioner: How Professionals Think in Action*. London: Maurice Temple Smith.

Waterhouse, S. (2004) Deviant and non-deviant identities in the classroom: patrolling the boundaries of the normal social world, *European Journal of Special Needs Education*, 19(1): 69–84.

# 6 Creativity and early years settings

## Anna Craft

Consider the following stories.

---

### Story 1: The cloud is on

Jacob, aged 29 months, looks up into the wide, cloud-scudded sky in Suffolk, eastern England, on a June evening. The sun has begun to set behind the clouds, giving them a luminous appearance. He says, 'Look, Mummy, the cloud is on' ...

---

### Story 2: Long swishy grass

Georgia (3), Jack (5), Steven (2), Sara (6) and Jon (7) are taken on a walk by their childminder one spring afternoon, through the fields close to her house, in the Midlands in England. They sit down to rest in one of the fields, in which the grass is long. There are no cattle or sheep grazing it this season. After a snack and a drink, Steven starts to crawl through the soft grass, which towers above him. Georgia and Sara follow, and soon all five children are making 'tracks' in the long swishy grass. The afternoon becomes known as the Long Swishy Grass Day, and the field as the Long Swishy Grass Field.

---

### Story 3: Following an idea

Erin, aged 8, finds concentration difficult, especially when sitting on the carpet in his classroom. The most challenging time is when his teacher is explaining some maths. He finds that his mind gets hold of an idea and follows it – so he loses the plot in terms of what he is being told. After one of these experiences, he explains, 'We were talking about the

9x table and I suddenly realized there was a pattern and my mind went off following the pattern and when I came back I didn't know what we were supposed to be doing. My teacher was quite cross.'

**Story 4: Daisy soup**

Eva (3 years, 4 months) and Zach (3 years, 6 months) are playing in the outdoor Play area of their Foundation Stage Unit, in a primary school in the north east of England. They find some daisies growing in the grassy area and they busy themselves with picking them, beheading them and separating out the petals to put into an empty plastic yoghurt pot. 'These are going to be a soup,' says Zach.

What do all of these moments have in common? A vital element in each is the sheer creative engagement manifested by each of these young learners, who is each in different ways moving beyond the given, or 'what is', to the possible, or 'what could be'. They are using, in other words, what might be called 'possibility thinking'.

## Possibility at the heart of creativity

I have long argued that 'possibility thinking' is the common core to all creativity in young children, whether alone or in collaboration/parallel with others. This is the case in any area of learning – for example, in cooking, imaginative play, mark-making or writing, musical exploration and composition, outdoor physical play, mathematical development or early scientific inquiry. Possibility thinking is the means by which questions are posed or puzzles surfaced – through multiple manifestations of 'what if?' (Craft 2000, 2001, 2002).

'What if?' can be a conscious question or may be experienced much more unconsciously in the flow of engagement. Possibility thinking is vital to 'high c' creativity (for example, in the work of a designer, or the creative engagement of a computer programmer), where a field of knowledge could be transformed by the creator. But it is just as relevant in 'little c creativity', at the other end of the spectrum (for example, in 2-year-old Steven realizing in crawling through the long grass that it starts to make a 'track', in 8-year-old Erin realizing that a number pattern can be made in following the 9x table, in an adult working out how to make a meal from an unexpectedly limited number of ingredients, or a pair of 3-year-olds making 'soup' from daisy petals).

Possibility thinking, then, involves a shift from recognition (i.e. 'what is this?') to exploration (i.e. 'what can I/we do with this?'). It involves the finding and honing of problems as well as the solving of them, a distinction that has been explored through studies in primary classrooms (Jeffrey 2004, 2005; Jeffrey and Craft 2004).

While possibility thinking is just as relevant to adults as it is to children, this chapter is focused on fostering *children's* possibility thinking. It is suggested that fostering possibility thinking builds their resilience and confidence, in reinforcing their capabilities as confident explorers, mean-ing-makers and decision-makers. So, how does fostering creativity relate to the wider policy context? Here we look at the case of England as an example of global policy development that places very high value on fostering young children's creativity.

## Policy on creativity in the early years

In England, 1999 proved to be a watershed in policy-making on creativity. In this year, the National Advisory Committee for Creative and Cultural Education (NACCCE 1999) advocated that alongside having high standards of academic achievement, young people now needed to leave formal education able to 'adapt, see connections, innovate, communicate and work with others' (NACCCE 1999: 13). Concrete proposals in the NACCCE report can be seen as having provided a foundation for other, more recent, educational policy moves in England, many of which have been implemen-ted. These included shifts in the wider policy agenda that influenced early childhood education, such as the introduction of *Every Child Matters* from 2003 (DfES 2004b) – a government initiative designed to ensure the well-being of children and young people from birth to age 19, by supporting the development of resilience and resourcefulness (Craft 2005). It also led to focused engagement by policy-makers and policy advisers, such as the establishment of the Qualifications and Curriculum Authority Creativity Project (QCA 2005a, 2005b), also the publishing by the DfES of the booklet *Excellence and Enjoyment*, for primary schools, in May 2003 (DfES 2003), exhorting primary schools to take creative and innovative approaches to the curriculum and to place creativity high on their agendas, followed by materials (DfES 2004a) to encourage this. In late 2005 and early 2006, a further government review of creativity and the economy was under-taken (Roberts 2006). It, too, led to change. From the early 2000s onwards, increasing attention was paid to creativity in the curriculum.

The introduction of Creative Development into the early years curriculum for 3–5 year olds in 2000 and the codifying of creative thinking skills in the National Curriculum for 5–16 year olds, was followed from 2005 by at least two key reviews. These included, as discussed elsewhere in this book, a complete review of the curriculum for 0–5 year olds, leading to a seamless care and education policy in which creativity was to play a key role.

These wide-ranging policy initiatives have focused on all phases of education from the early years through to higher education. And yet, common across them is the commitment to 'little c' creativity (Craft 2000, 2001, 2002) – that is, everyday, lifewide creativity as well as the creativity inherent within domains studied as subjects in schools. There is a democratic assumption built in to much of the policy work stemming from the NACCCE report (1999) in suggesting that everyone can be creative in multiple domains at an everyday level, if nurtured and encouraged to be so. It is suggested that we are all capable of creative engagement, and that all learning involves elements of creativity. And, in *Curriculum Guidance for the Foundation Stage* (QCA/DfEE 2000), it is firmly suggested that creativity starts, as I suggested earlier, with generating questions, as follows:

> [creativity] begins with curiosity and involves children in exploration and experimentation ... they draw upon their imagination and originality. They make decisions, take risks and plan with ideas ... if they are to be truly creative, children need the freedom to develop their ideas and the support of adults (QCA/DfEE 2000: 118)

## Cultivating creativity: Creative practice and practice that fosters creativity

In her work on creativity with babies and toddlers, Tina Bruce discusses the idea of 'cultivating' creativity. She uses it in the way that Vygotsky (1978), the Russian psychologist, did in the late twentieth century – so as to emphasize that it is important for adults to support rather than to impose, and to nourish curiosity from within rather than imposing learning from beyond. She also acknowledges what a vital role adults play in the early years, arguing that without sensitive engagement with children and with their families, 'emergent possibilities for creativity that are in every child do not develop or can be quickly extinguished' (Bruce 2004: 12). I would argue that this is as true for older children as it is for babies and toddlers. As adults in early years settings, there are opportunities to develop our practice so as to foster children's creativity, by focusing on each child's motivations and interests, and in valuing and appreciating these, encouraging exploration without, as Bruce puts it, 'invading the child's creative idea or taking it over' (2004: 25).

It's important to recognize how creativity is relevant across all aspects of learning, as Beetlestone (1998) and Duffy (2006) remind us. It is as relevant in mathematics as it is in art, it is as relevant in imaginative play as it is in solving a dispute in the playground or generating ideas in design and technology. It is as relevant in exploring textures in paint, dried pasta and sand as it is in working out how to make the next game come up on the computer. It is also relevant across life, as I argue elsewhere (Craft 2002).

In reflecting on our practice in early years settings, we can distinguish between creative practice (imaginative approaches to how we work with children) and practice that fosters creativity (where our main concern is ensuring that we encourage children's ideas and possibilities, and that we don't block these). Such ideas are developed by Craft and Jeffrey (2004), drawing on studies undertaken in English nursery and KS1 classrooms (Jeffrey and Craft 2003). Craft and Jeffrey (2004) suggest practice that fosters children's creativity is 'learner inclusive' – in other words, open to hearing children's perspectives on their learning, and really taking their ideas seriously. It involves children and teachers engaging closely together – what Craft and Jeffrey call 'co-participation' in the learning context.

This close interplay between children and adults has been documented in recent research work in a small number of classrooms in England with children aged 3–7 (Burnard *et al.* 2006; Cremin *et al.* 2006). The study involved working with staff in three separate settings to investigate both their pedagogic practices and children's learning. The research team identified a number of distinct but interlinked core features[1] of learners' and teachers' engagement that are valued and fostered in each setting, in the context of an enabling environment, as follows.

- *Posing questions:* the team documented children's questions – both those that were actually posed aloud and others that were implied through children's actions. 'Invisible' questions, as we came to call them, were documented through close observation of the behaviours of young children together with a concerned, deep knowledge of each

[1] Thanks are due to my research partners in this project – Teresa Cremin (Open University), Pamela Burnard (Cambridge University) and Kerry Chappell (University of Exeter) as well as Susanne Jasilek, consultant researcher to the Open University, Anne Meredith, consultant researcher to the Open University, Bernadette Duffy and Ruth Hanson (Thomas Coram Early Childhood Centre, London), Jean Keene and Lindsay Haynes (Cunningham Hill Infant school, Hertfordshire), Dawn Burns (Hackleton Primary School, Northamptonshire) – for their contributions to the analysis summarized here.

as an individual. Teachers of young children in these settings frequently modelled out-loud questioning, as if to show children how much they valued them posing their own questions and, in this way, developing their own ideas. Children's questions were treated with respect and interest. We recorded lots of unusual questions posed by children, and being celebrated by staff as well as by other learners. Posing questions often involved imaginative playful thinking, so that children were in an 'as if' space (counting out the treasure 'as if' they were in an underwater adventure, for example).

- *Play:* children in these settings were offered opportunities to play over extended periods of time, and play opportunities were returned to and revisited frequently. The provision of extended time allowed children's ideas to develop and to combine with one another and with available materials. Children often travelled far in their play, highly motivated by their own interests and knowledge. They were often highly engaged, deeply interested and very serious in their playfulness, engaging closely with one another's ideas and experience, imagining all kinds of scenes, and encountering and solving problems. They were clearly highly engaged and what we documented reflected what Sylva *et al.* (1986) called 'high levels of cognitive challenge'.

- *Immersion:* the children were deeply immersed in a loving environment in each setting. The importance of the environment providing love and support is also highlighted by Bruce (2004), as well as by writers from the psychoanalytic tradition (Freud 1914; Winnicott 1971), who argued that allowing ideas to come spontaneously from inside exposes the child (and adults too) to levels of insecurity and possible anxiety in the moment of encounter with something new, so that particular care has to be taken to make the situation as free from criticism and mockery as possible.[2] The provision of a caring, positive and benign environment in each classroom studied was notable. And yet in each case there was also overt cognitive challenge involved. As Sylva *et al.* (1986) noted in their research, conducted in Oxford, this occurs when children's activity is 'novel, creative, imaginative, productive, cognitively complex, involving the combination of several elements ... is deeply engrossed'. The parallels between the studies are notable in this respect.

- *Innovation:* children in these three settings made strong and playful connections between ideas in their own ways, and were encouraged to do this. In doing so they were able to make knowledge of their own. The adults working with them closely observed changes in each

---

[2] With grateful thanks to John Keene for his insights on this point.

child's thinking, through their talk and behaviours. They explored and developed further the children's growing understandings and they offered provocations to stimulate the children's connection-making.

- *Being imaginative:* both imagining and being imaginative were seen extensively in these classrooms. Children imagined what might be, and adopted, often inventing imaginary worlds. Through their imaginations, children were able to be decision-makers about the quality of ideas, content of their learning tasks and ways of conducting them.
- *Self-determination and risk-taking:* children's deep involvement was encouraged. Children were enabled in taking risks, working in safe, secure and supportive environments in which they were expected to exercise independence (agency) in making decisions and where their contributions were valued. The adults supporting children's learning encouraged learning from experience as both empowering and generative, providing a safe, known and trusted environment – enabling children to move with confidence into original and creative spaces, and to take risks. An element of this was use of time. Each adult tried very hard not to rush the children.

## Enabling children by valuing their creative potential

The study also highlighted the significance of the *enabling context* in the classroom setting and wider school environment. Each of the settings in the study supported the playfulness of teachers and children, and encouraged self-confidence and self-esteem. This supported young children in asking a variety of kinds of questions and developing their tendency to learn creatively, through possibility thinking (Burnard *et al.* 2006). The adults in the settings intentionally valued children's 'agency' – that is, children's abilities to have ideas and see these through into actions. They assumed and encouraged children's motivation – which Laevers (1993) and, later, Pascal and Bertram (1997), demonstrated was vital to high engagement as an indicator of quality learning in early childhood education. The practitioners in our study offered children time and space to have ideas and see these through, and they stepped back to enable the children's activity to lead their support of learning. Figure 6.1 (overleaf) shows these elements of possibility thinking in the early years classroom, within one diagram.

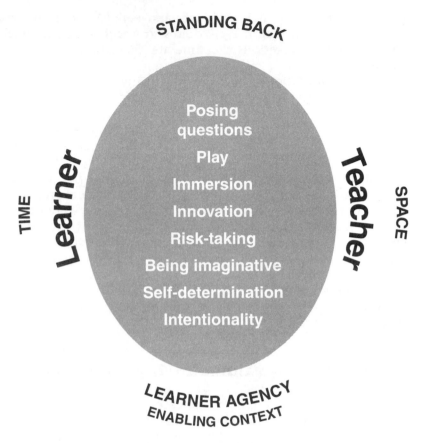

**Figure 6.1:** Adults' approaches to possibility thinking
*Source:* Cremin *et al.* (2006: 108–119)

## The dilemma of structure and freedom

As we develop our practice, we are faced with dilemmas involved in fostering children's creativity. These include *how to get the balance right between structure and freedom* in opportunities offered to children.

Too much structure can restrict the self-determination of children's own ideas (such as the 'template approach' to making a flower for display purposes, or for Mother's Day, for example, where every child is issued with an identical piece of pre-folded card and some coloured tissue paper cut up into small squares, and their job is to scrunch up the pieces of tissue so as to produce an identikit flower to take home or put on display, with no individuality in it at all). These kinds of restrictions lead to children feeling locked out of their own creative process, as witnessed by one 7-year-old girl who refused to give her mother the Mother's Day card made at school because 'we were only allowed to do it the way the teacher said' (i.e. by sticking pre-made petals, in a specific pattern, on to pre-formed, one-colour card, inside which the children were all told to copy the same message aside from their own name). This particular child made another card at home in time for the special day.

On the other hand, total freedom can be confusing. Sometimes it is helpful to suggest some limitations in the way we organize a space – for example, putting some resources out in the making area but not others – or requiring a limit on the number of people who may work in a space – for example, the home corner in a nursery or infant classroom. Finding the right balance is not easy; it is only by noticing how children respond, documenting and reflecting on this alone and with others, that we adjust our practice accordingly and work towards a balance that is appropriate to a particular child or group of children.

But finding the right balance is vital. Without it, Erin, who featured in the third story at the start of this chapter, will continue to lose the plot during carpet-based maths explanations. His teacher needs to learn how to travel with him, how to invite him to share the journey of his ideas, and how to celebrate this rather than berating him and locking him out of the creative learning process. The right balance enables children to make daisy petal soup, to make connections between electric lights and clouds, as in Jacob's 'the clouds are on', and to discover trails in the long swishy grass.

## The problem of culture in creativity

In England, as in many other parts of the world, creativity has, since the late 1990s, been increasingly recognized as significant in early years and other learning contexts (Jeffrey and Craft 2001; Craft 2005). Much policy development has been located in relation to both economic and cultural development (Bentley 1998; Seltzer and Bentley 1999; Jeffery 2005), making this a distinctive approach to creativity in learning as compared with previous periods where attention was paid to it (Craft 2002).

As I discuss elsewhere (Craft 2007, in press), current policy perspectives on creativity, then, see it as developing hand in hand with cultural development, both feeding from, and helping develop, the economy. The case is made explicit in policy initiatives in many parts of the world, including Australia (Australia Council for the Arts 2005), Canada (as discussed by Woods 2002), the Far East (Hong Kong and China are discussed by Cheng and Chan 2002 and Cheng 2004a, 2004b; the Far East and Pacific Rim by Fryer 2003, Ng 2003 and Lau *et al.* 2004 and Hill 2006). Concern is just as intense in the United States (Cultural Commission 2005), northern, southern and central Europe (International Federation of Arts Council and Culture Agencies 2005) and the Middle East – for example, Qatar (Supreme Council of Information and Communication Technology 2006).

However, while the cultural dimension, is recognized, and indeed funded and supported in various ways, in England (QCA 2005a, 2005b; Creative Partnerships 2006), the link between creativity and culture is seen as unproblematic. Not only is the model of creativity a westernized one, placing high value on innovation, on standing out from the crowd and therefore on individuality, but it is also based on a capitalist economic system. As Ng (2001) and others have shown, this contrasts deeply with what is valued in the much more collectivist orientation in Far Eastern cultures. This raises questions for practitioners working in multicultural environments, as I have argued elsewhere (Craft 2006; in press a, b). It also raises dilemmas for staff making constructive and collaborative links with parents.

## Implications of possibility thinking for reflective practice

The practices of children and teachers documented in the studies described earlier, emphasize co-participation and a learner-inclusive approach, as vital to fostering children's creativity. The practices involved a deep respect for fostering children's perspectives on the part of practitioners. These approaches are very similar to those documented in the Reggio Emilia pre-schools of northern Italy, which enable children to be involved collabora-tively, in relationship with both other children and adults working with them, in the sharing and creation of knowledge (Woods and Jeffrey 1996; Jeffrey and Woods 2003).

Researchers argue that creativity is fostered effectively through learner-inclusive approaches because as the child contributes to the uncovering of knowledge they take ownership of it. When control over the investigation of knowledge is handed back to the child (Jeffrey and Craft 2004) they have the opportunity and authority to be innovative. A learner-inclusive approach, then, includes children in determining what is to be investigated, and values their experiences, their imagination and their evaluation (Jeffrey 2001). It involves children experimenting and playing with ideas (Craft 2002). As children become more and more involved, the degree of inclusion increases. While the studies described here were all based in classrooms of one kind or another, it seems likely that the messages about possibility thinking, and how we foster it successfully, are just as relevant outside of the classroom and in other settings such as the home, playgroup, daycare centre, extended school, and so on. And it has been suggested, throughout this chapter, that what lies right at the heart of creativity, for children and for adults, is possibility thinking – the moment of transformation from what is, to what might be.

So what could this all mean for the reflective practitioner? Perhaps there are four rather vital and practical implications, which we might think of as building blocks.

First, it means *standing back* and considering what children are telling us through their engagement with the world around them. It means being alert to Jacob's description of the clouds being 'on', it means noticing the daisy soup, and it means celebrating the collaboration of playful ideas, which led to the tracks in the long swishy grass.

Second, it means *documenting these moments* in some way, as a mental snapshot, as actual still or moving images, as notes or, in special circumstances, as recordings that may later be played back. And, as Eglinton (2003) notes (in writing about how we document art in the early years – however, her remarks seem relevant to any discipline), we need to find ways of documenting dialogue, between children, between a child and member of staff, the dialogue a child has with her/himself during an experience, dialogue in the group, dialogue during artistic experience, dialogue during reflection upon work. Our documentation enables us to note and respond to pertinent events, responses and comments.

Third, it means *reflecting on what we learn from both standing back and documenting*, in order to appropriately support and stimulate their learning. Standing back, however, also means being deeply engaged with children's learning, responsive to their ideas, engaging in what Schön (1987) called reflection in action.

Fourth, it often means *working with others* – both the children themselves and other adults in the setting, where that is possible, to share perspectives on what is being observed. These last two – documenting and working with others – may be blended, in that documenting learning may be done by children as much as by adults and this shared in discussion in order to take the appropriate (and motivating) next steps in learning. It is important to consider what is done with documentation, and how it might form part of a shared record. Strategies often used include wall space, learning logs or portfolios, and home–school records. The main point is that in each case multiple ownership is encouraged, in making and using the record of learning. Working with other adults in particular also goes some way towards starting a conversation that might show differences in opinion, raised during the discussion on creativity and culture earlier, about the value of creativity and the purposes of it, both among staff but also between staff/practitioners and parents.

## Summing up

In this chapter, the notion of possibility thinking as being at the heart of creativity has been explored. Ways in which practitioners may support children's idea-making, and their 'what if?' questions have been discussed, and suggestions made about how and why this is important. At a time when creativity is increasingly being seen as a vital disposition in adult life, in surviving and thriving in an increasingly uncertain and rapidly changing world, and one in which creativity is being seen as perhaps unproblematic (Craft *et al.* in press; Craft, in press b), the need to develop our reflective practice to encourage and nurture possibility thinking in young children seems unquestionable.

## References

Australia Council for the Arts (2005) *Education and the Arts Strategy, 2004–7.* Surrey Hills, Australia: Australia Council for the Arts, http://www.ozco.-gov.au/ (accessed 29 November 2005).

Beetlestone, F. (1998) *Creative Children, Imaginative Teaching.* Buckingham: Open University Press.

Bentley, T. (1998) *Learning Beyond the Classroom.* London and New York: Routledge.

Bruce, T. (2004) *Cultivating Creativity in Babies, Toddlers and Young Children.* London: Hodder & Stoughton Educational.

Burnard, P., Craft, A., Cremin, T. *et al.* (2006) Possibility thinking, *International Journal of Early Years Education*, 14(3), October: 243–262.

Cheng, M.Y.V. (2004a) Progress from traditional to creativity education in Chinese societies, in S. Lau, A.N.N. Hui and G.Y.C. Ng (eds) *Creativity: When East Meets West.* Singapore: World Scientific Publishing Co. Pte. Ltd: 137–168.

Cheng, M.Y.V. (2004b). Developing physics learning activities for fostering creativity in Hong Kong context, *Asia-Pacific Forum on Science Learning and Teaching*, 5(2) (online).

Cheng, M.Y.V. and Chan, C.L. (2002) Teacher creativity in Hong Kong and its relating factors (Chinese), in, M.Y.V. Cheng (ed.) *Development of Creativity in Teaching.* Hong Kong: Ming Pao Publications Ltd: 211–223.

Craft, A. (2000) *Creativity Across the Primary Curriculum.* London: Routledge.

Craft, A. (2001) Little c creativity, in A. Craft, B. Jeffrey and M. Leibling (eds) *Creativity in Education.* London: Continuum.

Craft, A. (2002) *Creativity and Early Years Education.* London: Continuum.

Craft, A. (2005) *Creativity in Schools: Tensions and Dilemmas.* Abingdon: Routledge.

Craft, A. (2006) Creativity and wisdom? *Cambridge Journal of Education*, 36(3), September: 336–350.

Craft, A. (2007), Possibility thinking in the early years and primary classroom, in A.G. Tan (ed.), *Singapore Handbook of Creativity*. Singapore: World Scientific Publishing.

Craft, A. (in press) Creativity and education: tensions and dilemmas, in A. Craft, H. Gardner, G. Claxton, *et al.* (eds) *Creativity: Using it Wisely?* Thousand Oaks, CA: Corwin Press.

Craft, A. and Jeffrey, B. (2004) Learner inclusiveness for creative learning, *Education 3–13*, 32(2).

Craft, A., Gardner, H., Claxton, G. (eds). (in press) *Creativity: Using it Wisely?* Thousand Oaks, CA: Corwin Press.

Creative Partnerships (2006) http://www.creative-partnerships.com/ (accessed 27 April 2007).

Cremin, T., Burnard, P. and Craft, A. (2006) Pedagogy and possibility thinking in the early years, *International Journal of Thinking Skills and Creativity*, 1(2), Autumn: 108–119.

Cultural Commission (2005) *Our Next Major Enterprise: Final Report of the Cultural Commission*, June, available at http://www.culturalcommission.org.uk/cultural/files/Final%20Final%20Report%20June%2005.pdf.

Department for Education and Skills (DfES) (2003) *Excellence and Enjoyment*. London: HMSO.

Department for Education and Skills (DfES) (2004a) *Excellence and Enjoyment: Learning and Teaching in the Primary Years*. London: HMSO.

Department for Education and Skills (DfES) (2004b) *Every Child Matters: Change for Children in Schools*. London: HMSO.

Duffy, B. (2006) *Supporting Creativity and Imagination in the Early Years* (2nd edn). Maidenhead: Open University Press.

Eglinton, K. (2003) *Art in the Early Years*. London: Routledge Falmer.

Freud, S. (1914) *On the Psychopathology of Everyday Life*. New York: Macmillan (original German publication, 1904).

Fryer, M. (2003) *Creativity Across the Curriculum: A Review and Analysis of Programmes Designed to Develop Creativity. A Report Prepared for the Qualifications and Curriculum Authority.* London: Qualifications and Curriculum Authority (QCA), http://www.ncaction.org.uk/creativity/creativity_across_the_curriculum.doc (accessed 30 April 2007).

Hill, M. (2006) Investing in creativity, unearthing the treasures of the mind – a new light shines from Taiwan schools, *Taiwan Panorama*, http://www.sinorama.com.tw/en/show_issue.php3?id=200459305006e.txt&page=1 (accessed 1 May 2007).

International Federation of Arts Council and Culture Agencies (2005) Arts and Culture Online Readers News Service (ACORNS), *Publications on Policy Development in Creativity in Education*, http://www.ifacca.org/ifacca2/en/

new/page04_publications.asp?whichpage=5&pagesize=20 (accessed 29 November 2005).

Jeffrey, B. (2001) *Primary pupils' perspectives and creative learning, Encyclopaideia*, 9, June–July: 133–152.

Jeffrey, B. (2004) *End-of-Award Report: Creative Learning and Student Perspectives (CLASP) Project*. Submitted to ESRC, November 2004.

Jeffrey, B. (2005) *Final Report of the Creative Learning and Student Perspectives Research Project (CLASP), A European Commission Funded Project through the Socrates Programme*. Action 6.1, Number 2002 – 4682 / 002 – 001. SO2 – 61OBGE. Milton Keynes: CLASP (http://clasp.open.ac.uk).

Jeffrey, B. and Craft, A. (2001) The universalization of creativity, in A. Craft, B. Jeffrey and M. Leibling (eds) *Creativity in Education*. London: Continuum: 1–13.

Jeffrey, B. and Craft, A. (2003) Creative teaching and teaching for creativity: distinctions and relationships. Paper presented at the *British Educational Research Association Special Interest Group Creativity in Education Conference*, 3 February, Open University, Walton Hall, Milton Keynes.

Jeffrey, B. and Craft, A. (2004) Teaching creatively and teaching for creativity: distinctions and relationships, *Educational Studies*, 30(1), March: 77–87.

Jeffrey, B. and Woods, P. (2003) *The Creative School: A Framework for Success, Quality and Effectiveness*. London: Routledge Falmer.

Laevers, F. (1993) Deep level learning – an exemplary application on the area of physical knowledge, *European Early Childhood Education Research Journal*, 1(1): 53–68.

Lau, S., Hui, A.N.N. and Ng, G.Y.C. (eds) (2004) *Creativity: When East Meets West*. Singapore: Scientific Publishing Co. Pte. Ltd.

National Advisory Committee on Creative and Cultural Education (NACCCE) (1999) *All Our Futures: Creativity, Culture and Education*. London: DfEE.

Ng, A.K. (2001) *Why Asians are Less Creative than Westerners*. Singapore: Prentice-Hall.

Ng, A.K. (2003) A cultural model of creative and conforming behaviour, *Creativity Research Journal*, 15(2/3): 223–233.

Pascal, C. and Bertram, A. (eds) (1997) *Effective Early Learning: Case Studies of Improvement*. London: Hodder & Stoughton.

Qualifications and Curriculum Authority (QCA) (2005a) *Creativity: Find it, Promote – Promoting Pupils' Creative Thinking and Behaviour across the Curriculum at Key Stages 1, 2 and 3 – Practical Materials for Schools*. London: QCA.

Qualifications and Curriculum Authority (QCA) (2005b) http://www.ncaction.org.uk/creativity/about.htm (accessed 29 November 2005).

Qualifications and Curriculum Authority (QCA)/Department for Education and Employment (DfEE) (2000) *Curriculum Guidance for the Foundation Stage* London: QCA/DfEE.

Roberts, P. (2006) *Nurturing Creativity in Young People. A Report to Government to Inform Future Policy*. London: DCMS.

Schön, D. (1987) *Educating the Reflective Practitioner*. San Francisco: Jossey-Bass.

Seltzer, K. and Bentley, T. (1999) *The Creative Age: Knowledge and Skills for the New Economy*. London: Demos.

Supreme Council of Information and Communication Technology, Qatar (2006) http://www.ict.gov.qa/en/WSIS05/PM-Speech.aspx (accessed 14 February 2006).

Sylva, K., Roy, C. and Painter, M. (1986) *Childwatching at Playgroup and Nursery School*. Oxford: Blackwell.

Vygotsky, L. (1978) *Mind in Society*. Harvard, MA: MIT Press.

Winnicott, D. (1971) *Playing and Reality*. Harmondsworth: Penguin.

Woods, P. (2002) Teaching and learning in the new millennium, in C. Sugrue and D. Day (eds) *Developing Teachers and Teaching Practice: International Research Perspectives*. London and New York: Routledge Falmer.

Woods, P. and Jeffrey, B. (1996) *Teachable Moments*. Buckingham: Open University Press.

# 7   Listening to young children: multiple voices, meanings and understandings

## Elizabeth Wood

## Introduction

Contemporary research and policy frameworks agree that reflecting in and on practice is essential to improving the quality of provision, and supporting professional development. However, the concept of reflective practice may be narrowly interpreted as a means of ensuring that teachers and practitioners are 'delivering' the curriculum and achieving defined learning outcomes. Wood and Attfield (2005) argue that effective educators need to be good researchers, and to develop inquiry-based approaches to their practice. Similarly, Rinaldi (2006) proposes that early childhood education should be based on a 'pedagogy of listening', which encompasses ethical and political commitments to children, families and communities. By integrating such approaches, Dahlberg and Moss (2005) argue that education settings can become sites for ethical practice, in which practitioners can confront injustice and inequity, and forms of domination and oppression. They can also challenge assumptions, which may be derived from their own professional and life experiences, and policy texts.

In this chapter I will demonstrate that the skills of observing and listening are integral to repertoires of professional practice, and that reflective practice can extend into critical engagement with policy, theory and practice, from which new possibilities for action can be generated. Reflective educators can become change agents and 'activist educators', who have the ability to transform, rather then merely implement policy frameworks (MacNaughton 2005). Such developments are particularly important in the context of *Every Child Matters* (DfES 2004a), because professionals have contrasting knowledge bases and ways of seeing young people and their families.

In the first section I examine the implications of contemporary policy frameworks for developing inquiry-based approaches. In the second section I discuss methodological trends towards incorporating children's voices in research, and the implications for practitioners. Vignettes from research studies are used to provoke reflective consideration of children's voices, meanings and perspectives, and how these can be used to develop ethical assessment practices.

## Policy directions

Contemporary developments in early childhood provision and services are taking place within a dynamic framework of policy, research, theories, and changing images of children and childhood. Three policy frameworks are relevant to educational provision and practice: *Every Child Matters* (DfES 2004a), *The Early Years Foundation Stage* (DfES 2007) and the *Primary National Strategy* (DfES 2004b). These frameworks can be interpreted narrowly to promote a culture of conformity to technical practices, 'outcomes' and 'standards', or more broadly to promote a culture of entitlement, empowerment and inclusion. Personalized learning and services, assessment for learning, children's well-being, the voices and rights of the child, are policy aspirations that are shared across integrated service providers – education, health, law and social care. Such practices also respect cultural and social diversity, and promote social justice by ensuring equal opportunities and equal access to provision and services. The development of integrated services is based on inter-professional collaborations, which have the potential for creating new knowledge bases, practices and 'ways of seeing' children and their families. Therefore all practitioners need to develop active listening and observing, along with a language of critique and reflexivity.

## Young children's voices and perspectives in research

Recent developments in research reflect a willingness to involve young people as research participants, and to access their voices and perspectives. These developments are supported by postmodern and emancipatory theories and methodologies, which recognize children's rights, agency and competences (MacNaughton 2005; Underdown and Barlow 2007). Children are seen as expert informers and witnesses, and practitioners in multi-professional contexts take account of their choices and perspectives. The role of researchers and professionals is to understand children's ways of representing and voicing their perspectives, by following their trails of thinking and meaning-making. Participatory approaches have also created methodological and ethical challenges (Wood 2005), not least because children are capable of challenging and resisting dominant discourses and power relations in classroom and research contexts. Drawing on their work in the field of special educational needs, Norwich and Kelly (2004) argue that eliciting children's perspectives is not just a technical matter, it also involves complex ethical considerations and contextual factors, including:

1. the child's and young person's competences and characteristics;
2. the questioner's competences and characteristics;
3. the purpose and use made of eliciting child and young person's views;
4. the setting and context: power, relationships and emotional factors;
5. ethical and human rights considerations.

(Norwich and Kelly 2004: 45)

Researchers are required to work within ethical frameworks in designing, conducting and reporting research; they acknowledge the socio-political context, and the power relations between the researchers and the participants. Researchers have developed more respectful views about young people, and more sensitive approaches to eliciting their voices and perspectives about issues that are of direct concern in their lives, such as their health, welfare, education and legal rights. Those concerns are situated in networks of influence, such as home and community cultures, practices and discourses. Two complementary principles underlie a contemporary rhetoric of empowerment: a belief in children's *rights* (including the right to be heard, to participate, to have control of their lives) and a belief in children's *competence* (to understand, to reflect, and to give accurate and appropriate responses) (United Nations 1989; Brooker 2002).

These principles are relevant to academic and practitioner researchers. Accessing children's thinking and understanding is pedagogically challenging because adults' perceptions of intent (particularly in play) are only ever partial. Similarly, interpretations of child- and adult-initiated activities may also be partial where defined learning goals and curriculum content are the main indicators of progress and achievement. Reifel (2007) argues for hermeneutic approaches to data collection and analysis, with researchers 'placing texts within multiple narratives, reflecting the multiple perspectives of participants' (2007: 26). In hermeneutic enquiry, '*texts* can be used to describe any number of productions: written words, oral discourses (a conversation, an interview), performances (staged, informal, impromptu), and works of art (language based or otherwise)' (Reifel 2007: 28). Therefore textual analysis in early childhood settings can capture complex and multiple meanings, and the contexts in which these are produced and negotiated. Small actions and interactions often have immediate significance for the child, and build towards increasing competence and participation. Such approaches are relevant to researchers and educators for exploring playful meanings and actions, for individuals and groups of children. Researchers (and practitioners as researchers) can go beyond the boundaries of developmental and curriculum goals, because observations can be used as texts for analysis, not merely as evidence of developmental milestones, learning outcomes and curriculum targets.

Multiple meanings can be understood through different modes of representation and communication, and not solely through spoken language. In relation to issues of power, Silin (2005) argues that a concern with children's voices should include a concern with silence and silences, and whether those silences are self-chosen or imposed by others. In researching equity and diversity in pre-school settings in Australia, MacNaughton (2005) documents the potential dangers of giving voice to young children in research, because this raises questions about relative power between children, and between children and adults. MacNaughton recommends that the following questions be asked in research (2005: 130–1).

- Which children's voices will come forth?
- What will the consequence be for each child who participates?
- How might one child's voice silence that of another?
- What can and should I do when the voices are racist or sexist?
- How might intervening as one child voices their knowledge enable another child to speak?
- How will I honour those children who struggle to make their voices heard?

These questions are equally pertinent for educators, particularly in the context of *Every Child Matters* (DfES 2004a), where there is a central concern with children's social and emotional well-being and not just their performance against curriculum targets.

Recent studies explore how listening to children's voices can challenge dominant policy discourses and practices in pedagogy, curriculum planning and assessment. These concerns are illustrated in the following learning story, which is taken from a study on progression and continuity (Wood 2002). Two cohorts of children were studied across one school year: one from nursery to reception (ages 3/4–4/5) and one from reception to Year 1 (ages 4/5–5/6). Liam's story shows how his teachers interpret his progress and achievements through the dual lenses of developmental theories and curriculum objectives. However, in conversations with the teacher and researcher, Liam reveals humorous and subversive perspectives, and his preference for activities where he perceives himself to be competent. The study took place at a time of policy intensification, with teachers being pressurized to 'raise standards' through prescribed pedagogical approaches and learning objectives in literacy and numeracy.

### Liam's Story: reception to Year 1

Diane (reception teacher) is concerned about the pace of Liam's development, particularly his problems with fine and gross motor skills, concentration and sitting still. In March, Liam is copying over Diane's handwriting and is struggling with recorded work. In contrast his oral language is imaginative and vibrant, as shown in Diane's transcription of Liam's version of 'The Gingerbread Man':

> To make a gingerbread man you need some crispy water and some ginger to make it tasty, and some cherries to help them stick on it and some milk to make it yummy. You make one with play-dough, you stick it on with PVA glue and put it in the oven.

Liam is 'much more interested in drawing than in writing', and in talking about (rather than recording) his work. His playful use of language is demonstrated in a numeracy session that focuses on counting backwards from five, using the rhyme of 'Five Little Ducks'. Liam is asked to draw five ducks on a pond, but draws four ducks. Diane asks 'Where is the fifth duck?' Liam draws a duck over the page and says 'It is swimming away.' In the plenary session, he shows his picture to the class and counts 'one, two, three, five'. When Diane asks again where the fifth one is, he turns the page to show the duck on the back and says 'Well, number four swam away', and tells an imaginative story about the duck getting stuck in quicksand, then the mummy duck came back, but was eaten by a fox, and the fox was eaten by a crocodile. Diane interprets this episode as Liam having partial understanding of counting to five, and plans further work before he can progress to numbers 5–10.

In a subsequent conversation with the researcher, Liam recalls that the fourth duck is missing: 'It's on the waterfall.' When the researcher asks 'How did you know what to do?', Liam describes the sequence of his drawing, rather than the one-to-one matching and counting:

> Started with the water ... and the duck's beak orange, and the body blue and the ... and at the front the ducks have got webs on their feet.

Liam continues to use stories to contextualize his learning, and as a subversive or humorous response to teaching. Diane comments that Liam 'has got a very good imagination'. However, she anticipates problems with writing because of Liam's difficulties with fine motor skills, although she notes his skills in drawing:

> ... there is a really lovely picture of a duck, and it always amazes me as to how he can do such wonderful pictures because his hand control is just awful, and he's got such a really awkward grip as well.

In the first term of Year 1, Liam is focused on tasks, and responds to questions, but there is less time for making up stories or responding imaginatively to tasks. He continues to interpret tasks in his own way, and performs better orally than in writing and recording. In the research conversations, he talks about his interest in animals, and remains proud of his drawings. He follows his own agenda, expressing the achievements and competences that he values.

In December, Susie (Year 1 teacher) reviews Liam's portfolio of work, and judges his progress against the teaching objectives in the National Literacy Strategy. Susie has difficulty in getting him to focus on learning objectives:

> This year he is more focused on individual words. He knows how to write some words – for example, 'I' and 'zoo'. He can write his name ... he can spell words, he knows that there should be spaces between words. He knows about direction, how to start a new line. He's put a full stop at the end of the sentence, so there's quite a bit of progression there.

Susie says that Liam is an intelligent boy who is being held back because of his difficulties with recording, behaviour and motivation. Liam's progress is good when he does what she expects him to do, but 'it's really hard to get him to do it'. Liam is easily frustrated, particularly in tasks that require fine motor skills. Diane and Susie see Liam as an imaginative, creative child who likes to go off at tangents, but this creates problems within the demands of the curriculum objectives. The more Liam resists and follows his own agenda, the more he is positioned as a naughty child who needs behaviour support.

Liam's learning story shows that he experienced and interpreted activities in ways that were not always understood by his teachers. For example, from observing and listening to Liam, the counting and drawing ducks episode could be interpreted differently. His knowledge about ordinal and cardinal numbers was so well embedded that he could play with the idea of the fourth duck being missing, while still holding its place value in the 1–5 sequence. In other words, Liam was able to represent a more sophisticated level of

choices made by individuals or groups of children may be biased in terms of culture, social class, gender, sexuality, ability/disability, which may result in unequal power relations and detrimental power effects of free choice (MacNaughton 2005; Ryan 2005). Play-based approaches may actually militate against equality of opportunity and equal access to curriculum provision. Thus a pedagogy of listening and observing can enable practitioners to contest their assumptions about play activities, and to challenge stereotypical and discriminatory practices.

## Using a pedagogy of listening to inform assessment

Detailed knowledge of children is developed through observing, listening to and interacting with them, across a range of contexts and activities. The processes of reflection involve mapping evidence of children's responses and performances across contexts, and building a 'credit' rather than a 'deficit' model of assessment (Carr 2001). In a credit-based model, educators take pedagogical decisions and actions on the basis of informed insights into children's competences, perspectives and meanings, and their unique interpretations of their social and cultural worlds. Pedagogical documentation (such as recorded observations, examples of children's representations and communications, video and still images) creates an evidence base that informs interpretive discussions between team members. Such professional conversations can ensure that decision-making takes place within and beyond curriculum frameworks, and that children's perspectives, knowledge and competence are acknowledged.

These processes are exemplified in the following vignettes, which were recorded in a Foundation Phase setting in a primary school in Wales (the Wales Foundation Phase includes children from 3–7, in contrast with the English Foundation Stage, which includes children from 3–5/6). Around 87 per cent of children in the school are from minority ethnic groups, with seven to eight languages spoken in every class. The whole school team was involved in an action research project to improve the quality of teaching and learning through play, with each year group team choosing its own focus. The nursery team focused on improving the quality of language in imaginative play activities. Episodes of play were video taped for around ten minutes, and provided data for professional discussion and reflection. In the first episode, a teaching assistant (TA) is playing with the children in an outdoor role-play area, based on the story of 'Little Red Riding Hood'. The TA is supporting language development by playing alongside them. This vignette shows what happened when the TA's interactions did not flow with the children's play.

*TA to Majida:* Hello Little Red Riding Hood. Who are you going to visit today – to see today? Are you going to see grandma? What are you going to take her?

*Majida to TA:* Buns.

*TA to Majida:* Have you? Look at all that lovely food for grandma. That is super.

*Majida to TA:* Grandma not in there, not in there.

*TA to Majida:* Pardon? Grandma not in there? OK. It should be the wolf. Who's the wolf?

*Rajiv to TA:* He's already in the bed.

*TA to Rajiv:* But he needs someone to talk. Can you talk and be the wolf?

*Rajiv to TA:* It's not easy. I don't know what to think.

*Rajiv leaves the area and the play finishes.*

This episode provided much interesting evidence for reflection, focusing on whether the adult really listened to the children's meanings and the flow of the play. The team realized that it is all too easy to slip into question-and-answer mode when trying to understand what is happening in play, especially when they have not observed the beginning and the development of the episode. When adults were present (in this and other episodes), children tended to say very little, and relied on the adult to take the lead (even where the bilingual support assistants were involved). Rajiv's final comment – 'It's not easy. I don't know what to think' – indicated that he did not know what was expected of him by the adult, and perhaps did not have sufficient knowledge to further develop the role of the wolf. Rajiv's comment also provides valuable insights into his play skills: he is beginning to understand what it means to play in role, but needs to do this in his own way. Rajiv also understands that play takes place 'in the mind' as well as in social actions and interactions between players. What is 'in the mind' needs to be transformed into action for play to develop. His play skills were demonstrated in a subsequent observation of an energetic episode of outdoor play, where he leads two friends in a 'Spider-Man' game.

> *Rajiv to TA:* Mrs L. I am Spider-Man. There are two Spider-Men and more Spider-Men.
>
> *He climbs the climbing frame, then gets a scooter and demonstrates jumping off the scooter while it is moving.*
>
> *Rajiv to Jamil:* Come on Jamil, we are Spider-Men. Spider-Man can do this. You do it Jamil.
>
> *This activity continues for a few minutes before the boys stop and run away.*

Observing and listening to Rajiv showed the team that he could lead imaginative play with friends of his choice, and that he was willing to talk about his game and demonstrate his competence to an adult. Play provides many opportunities for 'out-loud thinking' as children reveal the purposes and direction of the action, and the imaginative context of their activities. By playing with meanings, they can also reveal quite sophisticated levels of understanding of their social and cultural worlds.

In a subsequent episode, listening to children involved observing their body language, facial expressions and symbolic activities, and, as Silin (2005) argues, listening to children's silences. Mohammed, a shy child, was reluctant to speak to peers and adults. It was difficult for team members to know how much he understood of spoken English, and how much he was able to communicate in his home and additional language. In the nursery, there was a 'three-way' puppet that was used to tell the story of 'Little Red Riding Hood' (the puppet could be transformed into the wolf, the grandmother and Red Riding Hood, to show each character). Mohammed approached the TA with the puppet, and she engaged him in the story. As she told the story, he revealed his understanding by showing each different character at the correct cue. After much encouragement, he did respond verbally (but in a very quiet voice), using individual words. His facial expressions and body language conveyed enjoyment and engagement with the adult. He was happy to participate on his own terms and was under no pressure to communicate verbally. The TA understood Mohammed's intentions and meanings through respecting his silence, while tuning in to his communicative competence.

This study had some valuable outcomes for the nursery team, particularly in informing how they could accurately read and interpret play activities. Interrogating these play texts, and reflecting on their own assumptions and beliefs, helped them to develop a collaborative pedagogy of listening and observing, and enhanced their understanding of children's interests, talents and capabilities. Their assessment practices became located within a process of understanding children as learners and players, based on sharing and building knowledge. The study also demonstrated how analysis of classroom texts captures complex and multiple meanings, and the contexts in which these are produced and negotiated (Reifel 2007). Even short observations (up to ten minutes) can provide much valuable evidence for critical reflection.

The vignettes in this chapter have exemplified how children create individual and personal responses within diverse contexts. Young children are not passive recipients of knowledge but are 'epistemologists' in their own right. Therefore a pedagogy of listening respects children's understanding of their identity and individuality, and helps educators to understand the influences of wider social systems such as class, culture, ethnicity, gender and sexuality. A pedagogy of listening also ensures that multimodal forms of communication are recognized and valued, and that children are not silenced by their inability to communicate in a dominant language, or within a dominant culture.

## From reflective to activist educators

Contemporary researchers and theorists have extended the concept of 'reflective practitioners' to 'activist educators' who see their practice as inherently ethical and political. A pedagogy of reflexivity is synchronous with a pedagogy of critical engagement. These developments are essential as educators work in increasingly complex contexts, with diverse communities and within challenging policy frameworks. Activist educators can transform, rather then merely implement, policies; they go beyond the platitudes of 'facilitating' and 'enabling' children's development. Instead, they work towards greater equity and social justice, and become co-constructors of vibrant communities of practice, which draw on the perspectives, meanings and resourcefulness of all members. They are prepared to act as researchers, to generate knowledge, to engage critically in their practice and to sustain collaborative professional development. These approaches will always provoke more questions than answers. However, activist educators will welcome such questions, in order to sustain their commitment to children's well-being and to processes of educational change and transformation.

## Points for reflection

- Use MacNaughton's six questions (see page 111) to consider critically your own perspectives, values and beliefs about listening to children's

voices. These questions may be considered in the context of a small-scale research project (e.g. for an assignment or dissertation) or in the context of your own practice. Discuss these questions with peers/colleagues.
• Carry out three ten-minute observations of play, and write a short interpretation of the children's actions and interactions. What do you notice about the text you have produced? Share and compare your interpretations with colleagues. What values and beliefs about children underpin these interpretations?

# References

Brooker, L. (2002) *Starting School – Young Children Learning Cultures.* Buckingham: Open University Press.

Carr, M. (2001) *Assessment in Early Childhood Settings – Learning Stories.* London: Paul Chapman Publishing.

Clark, A. and Moss, P. (2001) *Listening to Young Children: The Mosaic Approach.* London: National Children's Bureau.

Dahlberg, G. and Moss, P. (2005) *Ethics and Politics in Early Childhood Education.* London: Routledge Falmer.

Department for Education and Skills (DfES) (2004a) *Every Child Matters: Change for Children in Schools.* London: HMSO.

Department for Education and Skills (DfES) (2004b) *Primary National Strategy. Excellence and Enjoyment: Learning and Teaching in the Primary Years.* London: HMSO.

Department for Education and Skills (DfES) (2007) *The Early Years Foundation Stage,* http://www.standards.dfes.gov.uk/primary/foundation_stage/eyfs/.

Fleer, M. (2006) The cultural construction of child development: creating institutional and cultural intersubjectivity, *International Journal of Early Years Education,* 14(2): 127–140.

Guttiérez, K.D. and Rogoff, B. (2003) Cultural ways of learning: individual traits or repertoires of practice, *Educational Researcher,* 32(5): 19–25.

MacNaughton, G. (2005) *Doing Foucault in Early Childhood Studies. Applying Poststructural Ideas.* London: Routledge.

Norwich, B. and Kelly, N. (2004) Pupils' views on inclusion: moderate learning difficulties and bullying in mainstream and special schools. *British Educational Research Journal,* 30(1): 43–65.

Reifel, S. (2007) Hermeneutic text analysis of play: exploring meaningful early childhood classroom events, in J.A. Hatch (ed.) *Early Childhood Qualitative Research.* London: Routledge: 25–42.

Rinaldi, C. (2006) *In Dialogue with Reggio Emilia. Listening, Researching and Learning.* London: Routledge.

Ryan, S. (2005) Freedom to choose: examining children's experiences in choice time, in N. Yelland (ed.) *Critical Issues in Early Childhood*. Maidenhead: Open University Press: 99–114.

Ryan, S. and Grieshaber, S. (2005) Shifting from developmental to postmodern practices in early childhood teacher education, *Journal of Teacher Education*, 56(1), January/February: 34–45.

Silin, J.G. (2005) Who can speak? Silence, voice and pedagogy, in N. Yelland (ed.) *Critical Issues in Early Childhood Education*. Maidenhead: Open University Press: 81–95.

Underdown, A. and Barlow, J. (2007) Listening to young children, in A. Underdown (ed.) *Young Children's Health and Well-Being*. Maidenhead: Open University Press: 154–162.

United Nations (1989) *The United Nations Convention on the Rights of the Child*. New York: United Nations.

Wood, E. (2002) *Progression and Continuity in Language and Literacy*. Paper presented to the United Kingdom Reading Association annual conference, University of Chester, July.

Wood, E. (2005) Young children's voices and perspectives in research: methodological and ethical considerations, *International Journal of Equity and Innovation in Early Childhood*, 3(2): 64–76.

Wood, E. (2008) Conceptualising a pedagogy of play: international perspectives from theory, policy and practice, in D. Kuschner (ed.) *Play and Culture Studies, Vol. 8*. Westport, CT: Ablex.

Wood, E. and Attfield, J. (2005) *Play, Learning and the Early Childhood Curriculum* (2nd edn). London: Paul Chapman.

Yelland, N. (ed.) (2005) (ed) *Critical Issues in Early Childhood Education*. Maidenhead: Open University Press.

# PART 3

# Leading-edge practice: a community of reflective professionals

# Introduction to Part 3

## Alice Paige-Smith and Anna Craft

The four chapters in this final part of the book explore the development of reflective practice and the notion of a community of practitioners who work in early years settings. The authors discuss a variety of opportunities and challenges facing the mix of professions involved in the lives of young children. They consider how reflection and research can enhance the role of the early years professional by enabling an exploration and possible change of practice within settings. This part relates the development of emergent practices to the evolving policy agenda for early years education and care, informed by *Every Child Matters*, the Early Years Foundation Stage, Early Years Practitioner Status, and the developments around a common core of skills for early years education and care practitioners.

# 8  Multi-agency working: rhetoric or reality?

## Caroline A. Jones

### Introduction

This chapter explores the notion of multi-agency working, highlighting the issues involved in effective work with children across universal and specialist services, and illustrates ways in which multi-agency working can potentially improve outcomes for children. The chapter begins by discussing the importance for universal services, in contact with children five days a week (i.e. school and early years settings), of working with 'outside' agencies, as well as the importance of those agencies working together with each other to support individual settings and practitioners who, in turn, can then provide improved support to children, young people and their parents or carers. It highlights the benefits, challenges and dilemmas relating to multi-agency working. It moves on to discuss the Common Assessment Framework, seen as a key vehicle for multi-agency working, which provides guidance on a common process to assess children's actual and potential 'additional needs', including a 'lead professional' role and guidance on information sharing. It concludes by summarizing the benefits and remaining challenges facing practitioners as they strive to reconcile professional differences in order to make multi-agency working achievable in reality.

There have been many attempts to define what is meant by multi-agency working, and a host of terms such as inter-agency, trans-disciplinary, inter-professional, multi-professional and multi-disciplinary (Sanders 2004; Lumsden 2005; Wall 2006) have been used. Terms such as collaboration, partnership working, joined-up thinking and seamless working are also associated with the idea of multi-agency working. Sanders (2004) discusses the use of 'inter', 'trans' and 'multi', pointing out that 'multi' means many and 'trans' means across. However, he suggests that 'multi' is more appropriate as it implies collaboration between more than two groups. For the purpose of this chapter, the common denominator is that professionals with an interest in meeting the needs of children and their families should be 'working together' and sharing information with each other, within the bounds of confidentiality.

The *Common Core of Skills and Knowledge for the Children's Workforce* (DfES 2005a) suggests that the children's workforce should be able to communicate effectively with each other by listening and being listened to. It notes that 'multi-agency' working refers to various services, agencies and teams of professionals working together to meet the needs of children, young people and their families.

The idea of different government or local authority agencies working together is not new, but the drive towards integrated working that includes the entire children's workforce across health, education and social care sectors, as well as early years and childcare, police youth support and leisure services under the 'multi-agency' umbrella, is more recent and involves dramatic changes in thinking and in working practices across the children's workforce. Whereas, previously, professionals working together tended to be somewhat haphazard, this is now seen as an essential part of the early years professional role. At the end of the day it is individual practitioners who, to a greater or lesser extent, are crucial to the process of multi-agency working, and effective implementation may well be dependent on the cooperation of those individuals implementing the policy in their settings.

## A rationale for multi-agency working

The drive towards 'partnership' working has gradually been replaced by the terms 'integrated' services, or 'integrated' working both enshrined in the notions of 'multi-agency' working, and 'inter-agency' cooperation, terms that have been used interchangeably in policy documents. The Children Act 2004, for example, required each local authority to make arrangements for multi-agency working through a children's trust. The intended outcome of the requirement for inter-agency cooperation was to improve the well-being of children and young people, and to protect their welfare. Integrated services are central to the *Every Child Matters* initiative.

Figure 8.1 illustrates that services should be working together at all levels – from national strategic to local authority and in the community. The new duties in Section 10 of the Children Act 2004 have been the key policy drivers for achieving change. Here, the key construct is that improved outcomes can be achieved and sustained only when agencies work together to design and deliver integrated services around the needs of children and young people. The Children Act 2004 requires local authorities and their 'relevant partners' to cooperate to improve the well-being of children and young people, and to safeguard and promote their welfare. Children's well-being is defined by the five mutually reinforcing outcomes set out in Section 10 (2). These are:

1. physical and mental health and emotional well-being
2. protection from harm and neglect

**Figure 8.1:** Integrated arrangements through children's trust in action
*Source:* DfES (2005b: 7)

3. education, training and recreation
4. the contribution made by them to society
5. social and economic well-being.

This approach represents a significant shift from the historical roots of agencies working together as a process limited to the field of child protection and, more recently, to special educational needs. This swing towards incorporating a broad range of agencies was confirmed in the term 'relevant partners' who are required to work with local authorities in the children's trusts. But who are the 'relevant partners' expected to provide integrated front-line delivery and where do individual schools and early years settings fit into the bigger picture? The relevant partners listed include:

- District Council – housing, leisure and recreation
- Strategic Health Authority (SHA)
- Youth Offending Teams (YOTs)
- Police Authority
- Local Probation Board
- The Connexions Partnership
- Learning and Skills Council (LSC).

However, the cooperation arrangements were intended not only to operate at a strategic level but at service delivery level. Section 10 (1) (c) states that other agencies engaged in activities for or with children and young people should be involved, including:

- children and young people themselves
- voluntary- and community-sector agencies
- not-for-profit and private-sector bodies – colleges, work-based learning providers, NHS Trusts, GPs, Jobcentre Plus
- childcare, culture, sport and play organizations
- families, carers and communities.

Universal services such as schools and early years settings were also seen as central to the drive to improve outcomes and were expected to be actively involved in helping reduce the barriers to achievement that lie outside the school gate. The statutory guidance suggested a 'strong case' for multi-agency working arrangements in and around places where children spend much of their time, such as schools or children's centres. Alternative settings might include village halls, sports centres, libraries and health centres (DfES 2005b).

The objective of multi-agency working is to provide integrated, high-quality, holistic support, focused on the needs of the child and family. It is argued that such provision should be based on a shared perspective, effective communication systems and mutual understanding:

> Multi-agency working has a valuable role to play in improving outcomes for children and young people. Collaboration between people working in universal, targeted and specialist services strengthens inter-professional relationships, stimulates trust, promotes shared vision and values, increases knowledge of local services, provides alternative and creative intervention strategies, and addresses a wide range of risk factors. This, in turn, facilitates early identification, early intervention and preventative work. (DfES 2005b: 13)

Harrison *et al.* (2003) consider the potential benefits of multi-agency working. They suggest that it provides a focus of energy and resources of different agencies on a common problem, and enables a coherent and holistic approach to services for children enabling common policy development. Not only does it spread responsibility, but it can also lead to increased access to funding, credibility and authority. Harrison *et al.* (2003) list the characteristics of successful multi-agency working as:

- involving more than two agencies or groups, sometimes from more than one sector and including key stakeholders
- having common aims, acknowledging existence of a common problem and having a shared vision of what the outcome should be

- having an agreed plan of action
- consulting with others
- having agreed decision-making structures
- striving to accommodate the different values and cultures of participating agencies
- sharing resources and skills
- taking of risks
- exchanging information using agreed communication systems
- acknowledging and respecting the contribution that each of the agencies can bring
- establishing agreed roles and responsibilities.

On the surface, some progress appears to have been made. Wall (2006) gives some examples:

- inter-agency assessments prior to statementing of children with special educational needs
- development of Early Years Development and Childcare Partnerships, and Children's Trusts
- establishment of jointly funded centres such as Sure Start and Early Excellence Centres
- increased inter-agency training.

However, while few would disagree, in principle at least, that there are potential benefits in working together to improve outcomes for children, it is important not to underestimate the complexity of creating multi-agency structures.

## Challenges and dilemmas in multi-agency working

Even an acceptable discourse such as multi-agency working is subject to dilemmas in that individuals operate within unequal power relations. Policies and practices are subject to competing resources, choices and priorities, and are, therefore, inherently political. A survey conducted as part of an evaluation of a local Sure Start Initiative confirmed that multi-agency working could disrupt existing professional and agency cultures and lead to conflicts. The establishment of common aims across agencies was regarded as essential but less straightforward to establish in practice. It pointed to a need for new roles to be made explicit, and the allocation of budgets remained a major challenge. It also suggested that information-sharing strategies needed to be improved and that practices to protect confidentiality were creating tensions (Aubrey 2006).

Professionals bring different sets of values and beliefs leading to competing professional ideologies. It cannot be assumed that working together is unproblematic. Powell (2005: 81) notes that 'multiprofessional practices can be viewed as a comparatively uncomplicated, shared practitioner construction of children and their families'; the reality for many families is that different professionals only see bits of the child and do not see them holistically. This failure can be expensive for service providers and irritating for children and families as they struggle to find their way through the maze of professionals, often having to repeat the same tests and conversations over and over again. Nicki Shisler (2006), as a parent of a disabled child, writing in a Sunday magazine, shares her experience of this point: 'Then all the different agencies we use have their own set of practitioners: education, health and social services all throw therapists at us. There's barely a week that goes by without me having to bring another new person up to speed on my son's condition and history' (2006: 10). Sloper (2004), in a review of the literature on multi-agency working, concluded that there was little evidence of the effectiveness of multi-agency working in gaining improved outcomes for children and families. McConkey (cited in Wall 2006: 158), writing in relation to children with learning difficulties, also presents a somewhat negative perspective:

> It truly has been a 'road less travelled' as each service system has forged its own highway ... Worse still, at times they have worked competitively rather than cooperatively, blaming one another for perceived shortcomings. And perhaps most seriously of all, they have worked in ignorance of one another's values, priorities and achievements.

Loxley (1997) emphasizes that, in order for successful multi-agency working to take place, there is a need to identify, acknowledge and confront such differences. If practitioners are going to work with other agencies this calls for a long-term commitment and a deeper awareness and understanding of the roles and responsibilities of other professionals.

Abbott and Hevey (2001: 80) noted that the recent explicitly multi-disciplinary nature of government initiatives and their focus on the integration and coordination of early years services require 'something more than benign cooperation across existing professions. These initiatives require a truly multidisciplinary response.' It seems that professionals can no longer afford to stay within the 'comfort zone' of their own profession. According to Lumsden (2005), the 'embracing' of other professionals, children, young people and their families is essential to developing shared meanings and to working in collaboration. The implication is that it is relationships between individual practitioners that will ultimately determine the success or failure of multi-agency working.

# A process of negotiation

Multi-agency working needs to be thought of as a practical, evolving process of negotiation and communication between groups of professionals, occupations, sectors, agencies and disciplines. At the level of an individual setting, it is the setting's responsibility to ensure that the provision meets the needs of children and to ensure each child reaches his or her full potential; for some children, this can be achieved only by input from several professionals. The most usual reason for statutory or voluntary agencies to work with individual schools or early years settings is to support and advise practitioners in working with children who have been identified as needing extra support due to a special education need. As Drifte (2001: 41) points out, this can be of benefit to all those concerned:

> Working with other agencies is an integral part of supporting children with special educational needs (SEN) and their parents. This cooperative approach also provides valuable support to the practitioner, who can benefit from access to information and records that focus on a different aspect of the child's development. The practitioner can also benefit from advice and suggestions about the management of special educational needs.

Multi-agency working suggests that the children's workforce should work in a team context, forging and sustaining relationships across agencies and respecting the contribution of others working with children, young people and families. The implication is that all practitioners should actively seek and respect the knowledge and input of others. Yet how can individuals in schools or early years settings forge shared perspectives with 'outside agencies', who at best visit from time to time and at worst may appear to see themselves as the 'professionals' on the basis of their experience, specific expertise and qualifications? In the early years context, for example, there has been increasing intervention of 'outsiders' over recent years (e.g. advisory teachers, area SENCOs and development workers), each with their own message and each taking up precious time. In order to take full advantage of the knowledge, expertise and skills of each agency it is essential for practitioners to understand the roles and responsibilities of those working within each agency. This, in turn, requires a willingness of those working in schools or early years settings to learn and accept the 'expertise' of others as an asset rather than a threat. This can be difficult to achieve where there are issues and possible sources of tension relating to differences in professional cultures, including attitudes, values, beliefs and working practices. The following scenario shows how easily tensions may arise.

Jack, a 4 year old with Down syndrome is quite small compared to his peers. He has spent a year in a private nursery on the school site, which is well known locally for inclusive practice. With the support of a key worker, Jack has been fully included in the life of the nursery, without any adaptations. His parents and the nursery manager assumed that his transition to the reception class would be smooth. The school, which wanted to admit Jack, was concerned that the chairs were too big for Jack and his feet would not touch the floor. The occupational therapist came in several times and Jack was taken over to the school to be measured and fitted into a special wooden chair, with straps to prevent him falling out. The nursery manager was furious that this chair would segregate Jack, reduce his independence (which the nursery staff had worked hard to promote) by confining him and would make him stand out as different, undoing all the work the nursery had done to ensure Jack was valued and included. She suggested a more inclusive approach would be to buy a few small nursery-sized chairs for Jack and the other small pupils, and a lower table. Jack was distressed by the interventions and cried every time he went to the reception classroom.

This example shows that multi-agency working involves a complex process of negotiation between individuals, in which communication is an essential ingredient. It highlights a situation where a simple visit to the nursery beforehand – observing Jack, seeking his view and organizing a discussion with the nursery manager – may have avoided embarrassing professional conflict and distress to the child and his parents. It illustrates the potential negative impact of leaving individual practitioners in settings who are not, strictly speaking, part of any 'agency', out of the loop. One initiative, known as the Common Assessment Framework (CAF), attempts to alleviate such misunderstandings and improve the effectiveness of multi-agency working by introducing the role of the 'lead professional' and establishing common processes for assessment and information sharing.

## The Common Assessment Framework (CAF): a multi-agency approach to assessment

Numerous statutory and non-statutory guidance documents have been produced following the Green Paper *Every Child Matters* (DfES 2003) and the Children Act 2004. A suite of five 'core' documents supported statutory provisions in the Children Act. Alongside these were numerous other key policy and planning documents. One initiative, known as the Common Assessment Framework, has gradually been implemented from April 2006. This framework heralded a renewed emphasis on multi-agency working and was seen as having the potential to 'drive multi-agency working by embedding a shared process, developing a shared language of need and improving the information flow between agencies' (DfES 2005b: 15). The intention was that if common assessment can be embedded, the majority of common assessments will be carried out by schools, childcare, early years settings such as children's centres, other educational establishments, health services and children's services including those in the voluntary sector. The CAF should help practitioners to develop shared understandings of a child's needs and to avoid families having to repeat themselves to various agencies. It is intended to be a high-quality common process, which acts as a basis for early intervention before problems reach crisis point. Certainly the CAF can be seen as a preventative measure as well as a tool to provide compensatory intervention before things reach crisis point. It can be used by practitioners who have been on training, to assess the needs of unborn babies, infants, children and young people. The statutory guidance accompanying Sections 10 and 11 of the Children Act 2004 set out the expectations of common assessment. It points to three key *interdependent* aspects of delivering better services. The first is the CAF process; second is the role of lead professional; and third, legal and professional information sharing.

The CAF is a generic rather than a specific tool. Other assessments such as universal checks and SEN remain in place. Common assessments are intended to be:

- entirely voluntary
- holistic, centred on the child and rooted in child development
- solution and action focused
- based on developing an inter-agency culture of understanding and trust
- an easy and accessible process for all practitioners
- transferable between services and areas.

The CAF process was based on the idea of a continuum of needs and services. As Figure 8.2 shows, the terminology is confusing in that children described as having 'additional' needs may require targeted support either from a single practitioner or a range of integrated services. However, children with 'complex' needs (who are still part of the broad group with additional needs), require statutory or specialist services. These children may or may not have 'special educational needs' that are 'educational'.

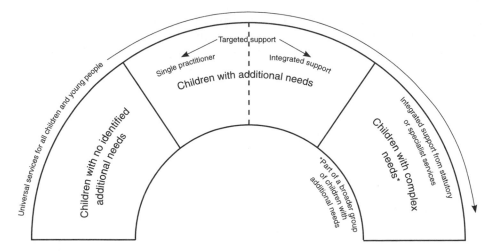

**Figure 8.2:** Continuum of needs and services
*Source:* DfES (2006a: 7)

## How to do a Common Assessment: preparation – discussion – delivery

The CAF process consists of three steps to be followed by the individual practitioner. The diagram in Figure 8.3 (overleaf) illustrates these steps. However, this simple representation disguises the complexity of assessment. To begin with, a practitioner is meant to identify a child's additional or even 'potential' additional needs without any clear definition or threshold explaining what the term additional needs means, apart from possibly needing services additional to those already provided within the setting.

### Step 1: preparation

The practitioner needs to check if anyone else is working with the child as a Common Assessment may already exist. This would normally be by asking the parent or carer, or there may be a local system for logging Common Assessments. If the practitioner is not sure whether an assessment is needed the CAF pre-assessment checklist can be used (DfES 2006b). This short form is available electronically; it is intended to lead to better understanding as to whether an assessment is needed – a decision to be made jointly with the child and/or the child's parent(s).

### Step 2: discussion

The information is recorded during the discussion with child and family onto the CAF form. It is essential to ensure parents understand what information is

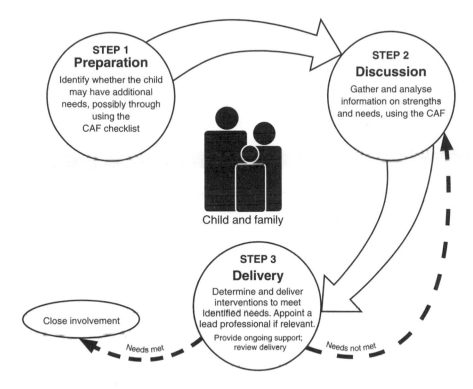

**Figure 8.3:** The three steps in the Common Assessment process
*Source:* DfES (2006a: 17)

being recorded, what will be done with it and when. The CAF form has eight stages with discussion prompts. The practitioner is expected to record a child's strengths as well as needs. The discussion is clearly organized into the eight stages listed below.

1. Explain the purpose of the assessment
2. Basic identifying details
3. Assessment information
4. Details of the parents/carers
5. Current home and family situation
6. Details of services working with the child
7. Assessment summary
   (a) development of the child
   (b) parents and carers
   (c) family and environment
8. Conclusions, solutions and actions

Stage 7 forms the core of the discussion, which is intentionally collaborative and based around the three domains shown in Figure 8.4.

## Step 3: delivery

It may be that no additional action is needed. If action is needed it could be by the family, within the service or setting carrying out the assessment, or there may be a need to try to access support from other agencies. Where it is agreed that the child has complex needs and integrated services are required the practitioner will need to contact the relevant person in the local area.

## Lead professional

The lead professional comes out of the CAF process where appropriate. Where children have no additional needs or where their needs require support from just one practitioner a lead professional is not required. If Common Assessment identifies a number of practitioners to be involved, a lead professional will need to be selected. One practitioner assumes the role of lead

**Development of child**

- Health
  - *general health, physical development and speech, language and communications development*
- Emotional and social development
- Behavioural development
- Identity, including self-esteem, self-image and social presentation
- Family and social relationships
- Self-care skills and independence
- Learning
  - *understanding, reasoning and problem-solving, participation in learning, education and employment, progress and achievement, aspirations*

**Parents and carers**

- Basic care, ensuring safety and protection
- Emotional warmth and stability
- Guidance, boundaries and stimulation

**Family and environmental**

- Family history, functioning and well-being
- Wider family
- Housing, employment and financial considerations
- Social and community elements and resources, including education

**Figure 8.4:** Elements of the three domains
*Source:* DfES (2006a: 20)

professional and takes responsibility for coordinating the action identified as a result of the assessment process. In some cases where a child's needs are more complex and they receive a specialist assessment there should already be a single point of contact who will assume the role of lead professional (e.g. named social worker, key worker).

## Information sharing

One of the key intended purposes of the CAF is to support better information sharing between services. The non-statutory guidance on information sharing intended for everyone working with children or young people, in the public, private and voluntary sectors, including volunteers, suggests that improving information sharing is a 'cornerstone' of government strategy to improve outcomes for children (DfES 2006c). Sharing information is seen as essential to enable early intervention so as to help those who need additional services, thus reducing inequalities between disadvantaged children and others. The guidance sets out six key points:

1. Practitioners should explain from the beginning of the process which information will be shared, the reasons why and how it will be shared. The exception being that if an open explanation would put the child or others at risk of significant harm.
2. The safety and welfare of the child is paramount.
3. Whenever possible, if the child or family do not consent to have information shared their wishes should be respected.
4. You should seek advice especially if you have concerns about a child's safety or welfare.
5. It is essential to check that information is accurate, up to date, necessary for the purpose, and shared securely with only those who need to see it.
6. Record decisions whether you decide to share information or not to share it.

(DfES 2006c: 5)

The potential for sharing information has implications not only for workload and time management but in relation to consent and confidentiality. One daunting factor is the sheer number of professionals with whom practitioners may have to work in education, health and social services, as well as the many voluntary organizations. The hub in Figure 8.5 (overleaf) shows key agencies working with children or young people.

This hub has 13 sectors and each has its own internal communication network. Although maintained schools have been required for some time to

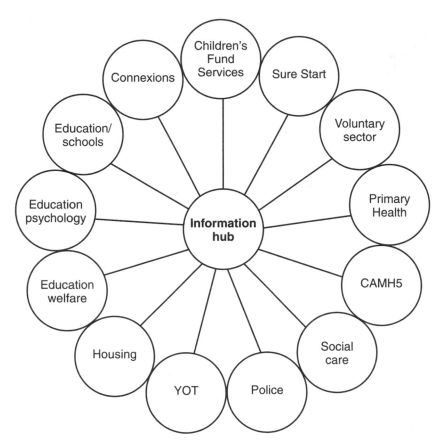

**Figure 8.5:** The information hub
*Source:* DfES (2003: 54)

publish information about their arrangements for working with health, social services and LEA support services, and any relevant local and national voluntary organizations, it is a huge task for non-maintained early years settings to find out who the support services and agencies are and how to contact them. The list below is a non-exhaustive example from just one private day nursery:

- community health workers
- speech and language therapist
- play therapist
- community nurse
- family workers
- educational psychologist

- child development centre
- general practitioner
- social worker
- specialist teachers (e.g. of sensory impairments)
- Parent Partnership Service
- Pre-School Learning Alliance
- Area SENCO
- development worker
- advisory teachers.

The entire process depends on parental cooperation and raises issues of a sensitive and confidential nature. The Data Protection Act 1998 does not prevent the sharing of information but sets parameters for sharing information lawfully. The professional would need to record and update the parental consent to share the information with others, preferably in writing. It is simplistic to assume that parents will be willing to sit down and have virtually every aspect of their child's life probed, discussed and recorded. In terms of confidentiality, professionals need to be made aware of the nature of confidentiality, when and why it is sometimes possible to pass on information without consent. This is a complex area and there are significant training implications.

## Evaluation of multi-agency working

The success of multi-agency working is continually being evaluated at all levels. Statutory arrangements are in place for joint inspection of all children's services in a local authority. Joint Area Reviews (JARs) report on how far services are working together to secure positive outcomes for children and young people. They involve nine inspectorates and commissions in assessing how social, health, education and criminal justice services and systems, taken together, contribute to improved outcomes for children. In early years settings Ofsted inspectors, usually visiting unannounced, also judge whether the childminding, daycare and/or nursery education meets the needs of the range of children for whom it is provided and how well the organization promotes children's well-being. The message is clear that the entire children's workforce should be working together at every level, with each other and with parents and families to improve the lives of children and young people.

Sloper, P. (2004) Facilitators and barriers for co-ordinated multi-agency services, *Child Care, Health and Development*, 30(6): 571–580.

Wall, K. (2006) *Special Needs and Early Years* (2nd edn). London: Paul Chapman.

# 9  Reflective family-centred practices: parents' perspectives and early intervention

**Alice Paige-Smith, Jonathan Rix and Anna Craft**

## Introduction

This chapter first considers the context for early intervention programmes (i.e. a variety of therapeutic and support services for pre-school children with disabilities or difficulties in learning and their families). In particular, the Early Support Programme (DfES 2004b), an early intervention initiative implemented in England, is considered, through an evaluation of parents' experiences of this service. We then consider how early intervention programmes based on a developmental view of the child can deeply shape and affect parents' and children's experiences. As the programme is implemented, the child's home becomes, in effect, the early years setting. The family can be seen as experiencing 'transition' from one set of identities, roles and purposes to another, overlapping set. We explore the experiences and perspectives of ten parents of young children with Down syndrome, and the implementation of early intervention programmes through considering a study that brought parents into a reflective relationship with their practice, through interview and reflective diaries. We explore issues in recognizing parents as reflective practitioners involved in a team of multiple perspectives and shared responsibility, in the support of children with learning difficulties or disabilities.

## The context of early intervention and approaches to children's learning

Within the English context of early intervention policy and practice the Department for Education and Skills (DfES) has placed an increasing emphasis on the education of children with learning difficulties and disabilities in relation to inclusive practice, improving partnership with parents and early intervention (DfES 2004a). This increased government commitment included the launch of a £13 million initiative in the form of the Early Support Pilot Programme in September 2002, as a part of the wider initiative of the Sure Start programme for supporting children and families (Paige-Smith and Rix 2006).

The Sure Start programme started in 1997 in order to support families, to integrate family support such as health and early learning services, and to provide high-quality integrated care. One of the main programmes for families of children with learning difficulties or disabilities supported by Sure Start has been the Portage service, which provides a home visiting educational service for pre-school children who experience difficulties in learning or have disabilities. Portage is named after the town of Portage in Wisconsin, USA, and was developed to support parents and their children in their own homes. The service developed there because parents found it difficult to get to centre-based services within that rural area (National Portage Association 2007). In 2004/5, there were 152 NPA-registered Portage services in England, with a total of 1194 Portage home visitors providing support for 5370 families through home visits and other related activities. There were at that time also 31 local authorities in England that did not offer Portage provision, and in four local authorities the Portage service was not offered to all families because of geographical restrictions. In addition, 1437 families were identified as waiting at their homes to be referred for regular visits from the Portage service (Russell 2005). By September 2006 provision for children with learning difficulties or disabilities had expanded to be encompassed within the work of 1000 children's centres comprising about 500 Sure Start Local programmes, 430 former Neighbourhood Nurseries and 70 Early Excellence Centres (National Audit Office 2006: 3, Value for Money Report Executive Summary). The expansion of early intervention services for children and parents within this context of expanding children's services, is documented in the report *Removing Barriers to Achievement* (DfES 2004a). This government document relates to the education and the inclusion of disabled children and other children with difficulties in learning. In 2006 the Early Support (ES) programme was evaluated by a team of multi-disciplinary professionals (DfES 2006). The report indicates that despite efforts to improve provision, the attempt to provide seamless support was far from borne out in practice.

- Many of the families had a disjointed experience with professionals from different services; some of these professionals were directly involved in ES and others had come into the home from other services.
- Multi-agency meetings happened in an ad hoc way. This should have been better coordinated by the Child Development Centre, which coordinates locally organized child health professionals (an example being given in the report of a parent having to coordinate a multi-agency meeting despite the presence of an Early Support programme).

The report also notes that:

> Another parent [23] told us about being part of ES but feeling that not everyone else who was involved with her child knew they were. She described the paediatrician involved as being 'on an island' and whilst the mother herself thought she had been allocated a key worker and thought she might know who it [the key worker] was, nobody had actually said as much to her. (DfES 2006: 192)

Other studies also document how within early intervention programmes parents experience anxiety about their own roles (Bridle and Mann 2000; Paige-Smith and Rix 2006). Such perspectives are considered to be affected by the type of contact parents have had with professionals and to what extent they feel listened to by them (Russell 2003). In particular, target-led, task-based programmes can result in tension and conflict between parents and their children (Rix and Paige-Smith 2005). However, parents 'teaching' their children more informally in the early years has been associated with progress in attainment in language, pre-reading and early number concepts (Sammons *et al.* 2004: 698). Woodhead (2005) refers to how Rogoff's (2003) framework of 'guided participation' provides a means to understanding how children are inducted into communities of learners through such informal methods. Development in such a context is seen as naturally social and cultural, as much as biologically constituted – a view of the child's development that contrasts with Piaget's (Donaldson 1986).

Recognizing the significance of social and cultural contexts in development in this way places parents at the heart of early intervention and underpins family-centred practice. Such a stance acknowledges the important role of parents in their children's well-being, health and education through partnership with professionals and their involvement with their child. Careful consideration of parental involvement within early intervention is perhaps particularly important for children with learning difficulties or disabilities, whose needs can heighten the demands made of their parents, as Beveridge notes:

> Parents vary in the personal resources they bring to their role. For example, their knowledge and understanding of child development, their communicative skills and their educational aspirations for their children are all likely to influence not only the nature of their parent–child interactions, but also their relationships with schools and other services. (Beveridge 2005: 42).

## Families experiencing transition of role

Families that go through the process of implementing early intervention programmes could be considered to go through a process of 'transition' in so far as there is an expectation on the roles of the parents to provide a structured education programme for their child. Supporting this transition process during early intervention entails effective management and a variety of communications systems 'to make the transition meaningful to everyone' (Fabian 2007). Fabian writes about the importance of certain activities that enable children's adjustment, not only in terms of their environment, but in the sense that there is a need to 'build a transition in children's thinking which supports the crossing between philosophical learning boundaries – from play to formal learning' (Fabian 2007: 12).

She suggests professionals need to co-construct such transitions with parents in a positive climate, sharing goals, values and expectations. At the same time she notes that it is important for children to be given some control and ownership of their transition so that they can have 'transition capital'. As Dunlop (2007) suggests, all of childhood represents a 'transitional territory between infancy and adulthood in which families have a part and can be social actors and agents' (Dunlop 2007: 157).

Transitions can be 'managed for and by children' (Dunlop 2007) through using a 'listening to children' approach. For instance, Clark (2004) has reflected on 'children's experience of place', which led her to develop the 'listening to children' approach that draws on three theoretical starting points:

1. children as having their own time, activities and space
2. participatory appraisal – the giving of 'voice' to children
3. the notion of the competent child within the pedagogic framework of Loris Malaguzzi, which sees learning as a collaborative process between adults and children.

An approach that recognizes the needs of individual children and their families could be seen as family-centred.

## Family-centred practice

Effective family-centred practice within early intervention could, then, include the principles of listening to children, as well as parents, alongside the coordination of coherent services. Carpenter *et al*. (2004) consider that equal partnership with parents and professionals provides an inclusive model of family-centred training that does not involve the transplanting of teachers' skills onto parents. He suggests the professional's role is to 'nurture the family, restoring for and with them their aspirations for their child' (Carpenter 2005: 181) in contrast to traditional parent education pro-grammes traditionally based on a deficit model (Carpenter *et al.* 2004), which may not recognize adequately what Woodhead (2005) calls a child's 'right to development'. Woodhead argues that government should promote children's optimal development, recognizing that early childhood settings and practices are culturally constructed, which includes the promulgations of belief systems about the 'proper' way for children to develop (Woodhead, 2005: 90), through the practices of the family: 'The way parents care for their children are shaped in part by their cultural beliefs (or ethno-theories) about what is appropriate and desirable, in terms both of the goals of child development and the means to achieve those goals' (Woodhead 2005: 50).

Counteracting negative assumptions and expectations within programmes that may be based on a deficit model should be a primary aim between parents and professionals, a process of engagement that requires reflective commu-nication – effectively, the development of collaborative reflective practice.

Russell (2003) suggests that partnership between parents and professionals requires them to negotiate different and new ways of thinking about situations and future events in order to reconsider expectations and plan accordingly. Parents' perspectives in the evaluation of the ES programme indicate that the family has to engage with professionals in order to access services and learn how to support their child's development. Early interven-tion programmes may be considered to be based on a developmental model of the child. Implementation prompts a transition for families who then need to work closely with other professionals accessing services and learning how to support their child's development, as part of a team encompassing multiple perspectives and sources of expertise.

## A close-up look at reflective practice in early intervention

The role of reflective practice in early intervention can be illustrated through a small-scale study undertaken by the first two authors (Rix and Paige-Smith 2005; Paige-Smith and Rix 2006), which involved two stages of interviews with parents of children with Down syndrome in England. It explored the following questions.

- How do parents, professionals and the 'child' collaborate and instigate pedagogy?

- What is parental knowledge of the child and how is this linked to the developmental perspective?
- How do parents use their knowledge with their children?

In the first stage of the study, informal interviews were carried out with three families, the parents of three children, including three mothers and one father; and in the second stage, six parents of six children were interviewed, one father and five mothers. The first set of interviews focused on the parents' views of their experiences of early intervention. The findings from the first set of interviews (Paige-Smith and Rix 2006) informed the second (Rix and Paige-Smith 2005). In the first set, with four parents, it became clear that parents considered early intervention to consist of a variety of activities such as yoga and play. They also said that they found it difficult to implement structured educational early intervention activities in the home and that at times this led to tensions between themselves and their children. Further questions were then considered, in relation to the pedagogy of early intervention programmes and activities, and looking at whether parents found that different approaches towards their children affected their experiences of 'being' with their children, in the context of early years education and care, which places an emphasis on the importance of play and creativity (Miller and Paige-Smith 2004).

As one of the researchers was himself also implementing early intervention activities in his own home, this added an extra dimension to our insight into the research process of interviewing. He was himself interviewed, reflecting on his own data alongside views and perspectives of other parents in the study. Analysis of the interview data was informed by this ongoing in-depth reflection, which occurred throughout the data collection process. Parents in the study were aware that we were conducting this research with one of the researchers being an 'insider', in the sense of both researcher and researched. Other parents in the study engaged in the reflection of their role with their child and reflective diaries were collated by two of the parents in the second stage of the research, which included the personal details and thoughts that the mothers had about being with their children. This data, alongside the interview material, was analysed according to grounded theory (Strauss and Corbin 1998).

## Learning together

Emergent from our analysis was a set of findings around how parents viewed their child when they were involved together in early intervention. The following discussion of the findings indicates parents' experiences when implementing early intervention programmes; some of these experiences relate directly to the early intervention activities. The parents' accounts also indicate how they perceived themselves and their role as a parent due to their early intervention experiences.

## The view of the child

During implementation of early intervention, parents and their children were expected to carry out activities that were identified after discussion with professionals. These activities were intended to move the child towards an agreed developmental target, and commonly involved some sort of teaching. One parent reported that she was offered 'tools' to learn how to play with her child, by a professional. The parents in this study were pleased when their child reached developmental milestones such as walking, talking, singing and drinking from a cup. Parental perspectives included a developmental view of their child through which they framed their child's behaviour and learning. Examples of this included one parent who said that, because she had read a book that explained the developmental stages of 'ordinary' children, she was able to predict what her child would be like when she would be older. The following comments indicate further how they framed the view of the child in relation to a developmental perspective:

> I'm always looking at what he'll be like when he's 3 rather than worry what he's like when he's 1 and a half

> Eva's gross motor skills have always been age appropriate ... Eva has always been cognitively age appropriate and remains so now at age 5

> As a parent, I think I compare him. I think what I do, sort of day to day, I sort of assess where he's at by looking at what the other children are doing. And sometimes I'm doing that with other children with disability and sometimes I'm doing it with typically developed children

Ensuring that the child 'fits in with other children' was considered to be important by one parent; another pointed out how she was pleased when her child 'gets the hang of things'. However, one parent also noted how difficult it was for her when other people judge her child:

> I think professionals sometimes forget that they are dealing with first and foremost a child, and then secondly that child has Down's syndrome, so that then affects on that child's mother, they don't do it deliberately, they don't you know, most of them are really good, they're very good at what they do, but you know, they do it so often, day in, day out that they forget, which is very understandable.

This view of the child could have a significant impact on the child's identity and self-esteem within a learning situation, especially if the child is viewed 'first and foremost' within developmental milestones. In this case, the label of Down syndrome seems to limit the perspective of the professionals so that they see the 'Down syndrome' rather than a 'child'.

The following perceptions of the child's experiences represent parents' perspectives about their child's learning at home and through early intervention activities. The parents considered the child would be:

- 'ready' to do activities – enjoys certain activities
- sometimes allowed to 'just play'
- instigate a song or a story, and the parent may respond
- get cross if others want certain activities carried out
- in a position that they would have goals set by parents and professionals.

The parents' perspectives on their experiences with their children perhaps demonstrate how they perceive their child. Their description of these experiences provides an insight into what it may be like for a child to participate in the early intervention process.

## Doing activities

Some of the parents described how they would carry out activities with their child:

> I would spend every morning with Richard for half an hour, 20 minutes, carrying out activities with him. And throughout the day, whenever I would do things, we'd try and interweave those activities into whatever it was that I was doing with him.

These activities would be measured within timescales, and were considered to be an important part of the day:

> I try to give her an hour every evening when we sit down together and we do various activities together. And then in the morning when she wakes up early I give her another hour then . . .

Providing this type of support was considered to be an essential part of supporting the child's learning experience:

> She has a lot of input at home, we simply don't waste an opportunity.

The home is considered by this parent as a place for the child to learn, and where her role is to support the child's learning. In the above examples the families go through a time of transition in terms of their activities relating to the child's learning and development. The child's experiences, according to these findings, indicate that the parents spend significant amounts of time supporting their children's learning through structured activities provided by professionals. Rix and Paige-Smith (2005) and Bridle and Mann (2004) have noted how there can be a perpetual 'tension' surrounding the expectation that there should be perpetual learning through activities. However, parental responses indicated that learning was not always through structured activities and that there were times that spontaneous play occurred, though often this was within play initiated by the adult.

## Playing

One parent noted how she was encouraged by professionals to play with her child:

> Just seeing the way she was interested in whatever the Portage visitor brought, she always wanted to know what was in the box, and had very definite ideas about what she would or wouldn't play with ...

Another parent noticed how her son enjoyed his play and had progressed to imaginative play with encouragement:

> Richard fed the baby [doll], gave it a bottle of milk and then self-initiated putting the baby to bed wrapped in my cardigan!

The importance of letting the child play was recognized, but the concept of play was interwoven with ideas around developmental progress and learning through play:

> She needed from me the ability to be able to play and she would often, she'd quite often, I think she needs time to rest as well, time to use what she's learning everywhere and time to just express it herself. So quite often I would find the easiest way to get somewhere with Katy was just to let her play ...

The child in these accounts seems to know or be empowered to choose to play or not to play; the parent's response was also to respond to the child's lead, which in some cases occurred spontaneously.

names. Learning Difficulty acquires its share of the children. (McDermott 2003: 295)

Parents' focus, then, on the evaluation of their child's progress in the context of both family and relationship with services, in relation to goal-setting. Whether the *child* engages with goal-setting could be a consideration of further research in order to establish whether and how the children are active participatory agents in the home setting when they engage in early intervention. Laevers' (1997) signals of engagement/involvement may provide appropriate and fertile indicators of the child's learning with the parent and professional (Arnold 2003).

## Conclusion

This chapter has highlighted how the relationship between children and parents in the early intervention process offers a 'window' on particular issues in reflective practice associated with parental involvement. We have sought to illustrate ways in which, in family-centred early intervention practices, parents too are early years practitioners, reflecting on their own child's learning, perhaps exquisitely aware of their own pedagogy. We have suggested that an alternative to the 'special needs family' that Bridle and Mann (2000) suggest can be created by early intervention experiences, might be practice that is more 'family-centred'. Such a family-centred approach should recognize partnership with parents, by professionals supporting and listening to parents and their children. As Carpenter (2005) notes, the notion of partnership within family-centred practice is in a state of flux, with high expectations being placed on parental knowledge and empowerment, or the creation of a 'professional parent' within a transdisciplinary team.

The process of early intervention consists of parents, professionals and the child collaborating and instigating pedagogy in the home setting. As Wenger (2005) notes, there could be considered to be a profound connection between identity and practice:

> Practice entails the negotiation of ways of being a person in that context ... inevitably, our practices deal with the profound issue of how to be a human being. In this sense, the formation of a community of practice is also the negotiation of identities. (Wenger 2005: 149)

We have considered how a 'family-centred approach' should include not only a focus on the family but also on increased and consciously reflective *collaboration* between parents and professionals in order to support the child's learning experiences. Parents' experiences of 'family-centred practice' within early intervention have been considered to be about the development of 'professional parents' (empowered with knowledge and information). The transformation the child and parent go through includes understanding more about the developmental view of the child, yet the challenge inherent in the developmental model is the implication of deficit in relation to the child who has 'special needs'.

## Points for reflection

- How does your setting involve parents in working with their child?
- How are parents encouraged to perceive their child in your setting?
- How could you enable your practice to be 'family-centred'?
- How would you be able to encourage parents to participate in their child's learning?
- What changes in your practice would you need to make in order to be able to 'listen to children'?
- How can you avoid the 'developmental' model becoming a deficit one for some children?

## References

Arnold, C. (2003) Sharing ideas with parents about key child development concepts, in M. Whalley (ed.) *Involving Parents in their Children's Learning.* London: Paul Chapman.

Beveridge, S. (2005) *Children, Families and Schools, Developing Partnerships for Inclusive Education.* Oxford: Routledge Falmer.

Bridle, L. and Mann, G. (2000) Mixed feelings – a parental perspective on early intervention, originally published in *Supporting Not Controlling: Strategies for the New Millennium: Proceedings of the Early Childhood Intervention Australia National Conference,* 1–23 July 2000: 59–72, http://www.altonweb.com/cs/downsyndrome/eibridle.html (accessed 21 December 2004).

Carpenter, B. (2005) Early childhood intervention: possibilities prospects for professionals, families and children, *British Journal of Special Education,* 32(4): 176–183.

Carpenter, B., Addenbrooke, M., Attfield, E. and Conway, S. (2004) 'Celebrating Families': an inclusive model of family-centred training, *British Journal of Special Education,* 31(2): 75–80.

Clark, A. (2004) The Mosaic approach and research with young children, in

Lewis, V., Kellett, M., Robinson, C., Fraser, S. and Ding, S. (eds) *The Reality of Research with Children and Young People.* London: Sage.

Department for Education and Skills (DfES) (2004a) *Removing Barriers to Achievement: The Government's Strategy for SEN.* Nottingham: DfES.

Department for Education and Skills (DfES) (2004b) *Early Support Family Pack.* Nottingham: DfES.

Department for Education and Skills (DfES) (2006) *Early Support: An Evaluation of Phase 3 of Early Support,* Brief no: RB798, September. Nottingham: DfES.

Donaldson, M. (1986) *Children's Minds.* London: HarperCollins.

Dunlop, A.-W. (2007) Bridging research, policy and practice, in A.-W. Dunlop and H. Fabian (eds) *Informing Transitions in the Early Years.* Berkshire: Open University Press.

Fabian, H. (2007) Informing transitions, in A.-W. Dunlop and H. Fabian (eds) *Informing Transitions in the Early Years.* Berkshire: Open University Press.

Laevers, F. (1997) *A Process-Oriented Child Follow Up System for Young Children.* Leuven: Centre for Experiential Education.

McDermott, R. (2003) The acquisition of a child by a learning disability, in S. Chaiklin and J. Lave (eds) *Understanding Practice: Perspectives on Activity and Context.* Cambridge: Cambridge University Press.

Miller, L. and Paige-Smith, A. (2004) Literacy in four early years settings, in L. Miller and J. Devereux (eds) *Supporting Children's Learning in the Early Years.* London: David Fulton: 124–136.

National Audit Office (2006) *Value for Money Report, Executive Summary – Sure Start.* DfES, http://www.nao.org.uk/publications/nao_reports/06-07/0607104es.htm (accessed 28 February 2007).

National Portage Association (2007) http://www.portage.org.uk/gen-Faq.html, (accessed 30 April 2007).

Paige-Smith, A. and Rix, J. (2006) Parents' perceptions and children's experiences of early intervention – inclusive practice? *Journal of Research in Special Educational Needs, NASEN,* 6(6).

Rix, J. and Paige-Smith, A. (2005) The best chance? Parents' perspectives on the early years learning of their children with Down syndrome and the impact of early intervention activities. Paper presented at the International Conference on Early Intervention and Developmental Issues in Down Syndrome, University of Portsmouth, September.

Rogoff, B. (2003) *The Cultural Nature of Child Development.* New York: Oxford University Press.

Russell, F. (2003) The expectations of parents of disabled children, *British Journal of Special Education,* 30(3): 144–148.

Russell, F. (2005) *The Extent of Portage Provision in England,* Final Report of the NPA Survey 2005. National Portage Association DfES.

Sammons, P., Elliot, K., Sylva, K., Melhuish, E., Siraj-Blatchford, I. and Taggart, B. (2004) The impact of pre-school on young children's cognitive attainments at entry to reception, *British Educational Research Journal*, 30(5), October: 691–712.

Strauss, A. and Corbin, J. (1998) *Basics of Qualitative Research: Techniques and Procedures for Developing Grounded Theory*. Newbury Park, CA: Sage.

Wenger, E. (2005) *Communities of Practice, Learning Meaning, and Identity*. New York: Cambridge University Press.

Woodhead, M. (2005) Early childhood development: a question of rights, *International Journal of Early Childhood*, 37(3).

# 10 Professional development through reflective practice

## Michael Reed

This chapter explores the way that policy developments over the past ten years have prompted an ongoing debate about the roles and responsibilities of the early years workforce in England. It considers how these developments have influenced the nature and content of professional development and in particular how this has led to a focus on 'reflective practice' within professional development. It also identifies a number of components and teaching strategies seen as promoting reflective practice for early years practitioners. The chapter raises questions about the way early years professionals may perceive changes in practice and policy, and considers how professional development may be enhanced by engaging in 'reflective practice'.

## The socio-political climate

Over the last decade early years practitioners will have found themselves in receipt of government directives, reports, policy initiatives and recommendations, all of which are intended to contribute to the expansion and improvement of early years care and education. A central focus of these initiatives has been the desire to support young children and their families in a practical and responsive manner. The expansion has included financial allowances for families to avail themselves of early years provision and the development of facilities to promote the welfare of children – for example, flexible arrangements for care before and after school, as well as the design and development of local children's centres. Such initiatives are now part of a culture that appears to recognize the economic and social importance of good-quality care and education, all of which has been driven by the desire to enact 'good practice', but at the same time placing high levels of expectation upon those most closely involved.

As an early years practitioner you may think that your 'professional world' is continually changing. You may even think that much of your professional life is involved in keeping abreast of current initiatives and responding to change. It is therefore important to understand how these changes have come about and perhaps understand the need for us to reflect upon such change.

In the mid-1990s the Labour Party set up an Early Years Task Force (1994) and produced a report (1997) that contained eight principles that would support subsequent strategies and initiatives. These included the view that early years care and education should be available to all young children, as should a range of services offering parents choice. Since that time, there has been a clear intention to increase the quality, accessibility and affordability of early years education and care. *Every Child Matters* (DfES 2003) highlighted the need for a trained workforce with newly developing multi-disciplinary roles and a childcare strategy (DfES 2004) set out the way government would deliver on the commitments made to transform the range of childcare services available to parents. In tandem with these reports was a National Service Framework (DoH and DfES 2004), which set out a strategy to promote a more preventative approach to children's health. It argued that a coherent strategy for effective joint working was of significant importance. These initiatives acknowledged the contribution made by practitioners and the part that they play in delivering such services. Indeed, the Children's Workforce Strategy (DfES 2006, 2007) recognized the critical role that the early years workforce plays in supporting the education of children. It argued that enhancing the qualifications of the workforce with more workers trained to professional level was an essential component of developing practice that, at its centre, has an emphasis on quality. This underlying premise was enshrined in the Childcare Act 2006, which is due to come into effect in 2008. It reinforces parents' expectations for the provision of high-quality childcare services and confirms the role of Local Education Authorities as leaders in partnership across all sectors. In addition, it lays down a curriculum framework and introduces the Early Years Foundation Stage, which will include literacy and numeracy frameworks for 3–5 year olds. It also includes a requirement for all early years settings to deliver integrated care and education in line with the Early Years Foundation Stage. To support these initiatives there is to be a new quality and inspection regime, and childcare settings for school-aged children will be judged against a set of common standards. Also planned by 2010 are a significant number of integrated children's centres (DfES 2005), offering 'holistic' provision that brings together early education and care. This is a significant development as such centres are to focus primarily upon inter-disciplinary and inter-agency working (Pen Green Leadership Centre 2007). The workforce is seen as a central component of such initiatives and it is intended to have a 'common core' of skills and knowledge that everyone working with children and families should be able to demonstrate (DfES 2006, 2007a). The common core sets out standards that prescribe what attributes and technical skills a worker should possess. The proposals also include conferring upon those with an appropriate qualification and experience – and who can meet a series of requirements and competencies – the status of 'Senior Practitioner' and 'Early

Years Professional'. There are also National Standards for the leaders of children's centres (DfES 2007b). In addition, the leaders of children's centres are encouraged to obtain a National Professional Qualification in Integrated Centre Leadership (NPQICL 2004). This qualification seeks to provide leaders/ managers and emerging leaders/managers of integrated children's centres with the opportunity to create an ethos of community partnership working, by coordinating high-quality services for children and families. This is an initiative that is of quite significant importance and places a considerable emphasis on reflective practice as part of its rationale (NPQICL 2004; Whalley 2006). Such initiatives are to be underpinned by inter-agency training and build upon such directives as the *Sure Start Children's Centres Planning and Performance Management Guidance* (2006, available for download at www.sur-estart.gov.uk). Details may change in the future but the whole framework reflects a set of agreed values for practitioners that promote equality, respect and diversity.

Perhaps this helps us understand that, for some time, practitioners have been responding to change, while supporting families and implementing a myriad of initiatives. At the same time, early years care and education has become increasingly recognized as an important part of the economic and socio-political fabric of the country. This has inevitably prompted a wider debate about the role and responsibilities of those involved in working with children and their families. Importantly, this has been widened to encompass a debate about the very nature of what qualities as well as competencies should be the province of a competent, adaptive, reflective practitioner. It is a debate that is an important dimension of early years care and education, and will have a lasting impact upon the workforce and the children in their care. This is a point underpinned by Osgood (2003) when exploring such change and in a recent series of articles with an editorial by Osgood (2006), which provides an informed contribution to this debate. The articles discuss complex and contemporary issues and raise questions about 'professionalism' and what this looks like. The authors address the issue of professionalism from a range of perspectives and they form a necessary antidote to the way that the workforce is sometimes seen as passive recipients of government directives. This moves the debate away from the notion of being an 'implementer' of competencies and technical skills, and makes us think about what is likely to constitute a 'modern professional practitioner'. Moss (2006) contributes to this debate and seeks to redefine the role for an early years worker. He suggests that this is a political and ethical choice that needs to start with critical questions about how the work of an early years worker is understood and what values are considered important.

What is clear is that significant change has taken place and that there is a developing debate about the role, responsibility and value base of the early years practitioner – a practitioner who is faced with a range of responsibilities.

It seems there is the need to have the ability to understand, interpret and enact government initiatives and respond to change. When doing this, practitioners should liaise closely with other professionals in their local area and develop positive working relationships. While doing this, they should be being responsive to the views of Directors of Children's Services. They should also understand the impact of regional 'childcare partnerships' and respond to the way Local Authorities will be taking on responsibility for local services. As they do this, they must understand the teaching methodologies associated with developing curriculum frameworks, and employ the technical skills necessary to organize and design children's learning experiences. In addition, they should monitor and reflect upon the effectiveness of these experiences, report information to parents and collate evidence in preparation for formal inspections. Finally (and no doubt not exclusively, as there are probably roles that have been forgotten), there is also the small matter of placing children and their families at the centre of inter-professional practice and responding to the needs of local communities – all of which would seem to require technical skills, adaptive skills, social skills, the ability to offer an analysis of practice, close inter-professional working, and the ability to respond and adapt to change. In essence, practitioners need to become competent, adaptive, reflective professionals. This point raises the question 'How might day-to-day practice alter when the roots of such change have taken hold?' It also raises the question of how it is possible to prepare practitioners for such change and equip them with the confidence and capabilities to meet that change.

## The role of professional development

With such changes in practice and personal perspectives on the horizon, it is not surprising that those involved in professional development for early years practitioners have analysed how to conceptualize practice and the 'reflective practitioner'. Professional development may involve the practitioner going beyond a demonstration of technical competence and being expected to engage in critical reflection. This involves exploring their own practice and the practice of others, and critically examining the way they respond profession-ally and personally to change, leadership, teamwork and working with children. Dewey (1933) suggests that we 'critically reflect' so that we can develop professionally and personally. In addition, the work of Schön (1983) is considered influential in offering a rationale for the importance of reflecting upon practice. More recently, Fowler and Robbins (2006) have provided a useful overview of reflective practice directed towards practitioner and mentor. Brownlee and Berthelsen (2006) take this further and provide a perceptive and careful consideration of 'reflection' as an aspect of professional development. Other commentators also subscribe to the view that reflection can deepen perspectives on practice (Buchanan *et al.* 2006; Manning-Morton 2006). Moon (1999a, 1999b, 2004) provides an analysis that focuses upon what might be termed 'reflective practice in action'. She contributes to the debate about how reflection can facilitate a clear understanding of personal learning. Bolton (2005) also offers valuable insights into the nature of reflection and moves us to consider not only reflective practice, but also reflexivity. This she illustrates as part of the dynamic between tutor and student working together, and suggests that students should formulate their own questions about the situations in which they find themselves (reflective) and the self they find there (reflexive). Moreover, she suggests that engaging in such reflection promotes a deeper understanding of actions that can lead to an improvement in professional practice.

## Implications for professional development

The implications of these changes for professional development are important. Reflective analysis may be beneficial to the individual and act as a mechanism to refine and improve practice. It allows different perspectives on how practitioners themselves view their own practice and permits them to consider not only the 'what' but also the 'how'. This raises the question as to what components need to come together to allow this positive interrelationship between theory and practice to take place. Of course, there is no easy answer to such a question and no readily available list of components. However, there is a growing number of commentators, some already cited in this chapter, who are exploring reflective practice as part of professional development. For example, the European Community Commission has funded a programme called the Reflect Project (2007). This intends to improve the skills and competencies of people in vocational training. It promotes the concept of 'reflection in training activities' and sees reflection as part of a continuum of meaning, moving from the functional to creative reflective practice. There are also commentators such as Craft (2001); who provides practical advice on design and implementation of professional development; in addition, Smid (2001) explores ways in which it is possible for universities to design learning opportunities and encourage self-reflection among participants, while Clegg *et al.* (2002) identify four typologies that illustrate aspects of reflective practice. Morley (2007) also offers an interesting perspective on the value of inter-professional training and considers how we might respond to some of the dilemmas inherent in engaging practitioners in reflective learning.

All of which makes us consider the components necessary to prepare participants for what they will experience when engaging in reflection on their practice. For instance, this may encompass aspects of confidentiality and a recognition that participants have to 'share' with others only that information they are comfortable in discussing. Any form of evaluation may be seen as linked to workplace evidence – such as informal or formal group presentations, or personal journal entries – which we shall discuss later in the chapter. Added to this is another component, which underlines once again evidence gathering in the workplace. This involves a formal recognition by participants that they intend to maintain an ethical standpoint when designing and carrying out any workplace investigation. Likewise, a recognition that confidentiality (as part of the investigation) is paramount and that sharing information adheres to professional propriety also seems to be an important strategy, especially when linked to assessment and articulated within written assignments. This moves the participants to reflect upon the way they have adhered to ethical requirements and consciously consider why ethical considerations are an important part of the process of reflecting on practice.

Another interrelated strand is that of participants actively recording what goes on in the workplace or what they perceive as important to themselves as part of professional development. It could be a commentary about their professional lives or perceptions about themselves and their practice. Importantly, it is personal to them and extracts are shared only when the participant feels it is important to do so. Professional development may be carried out via a reflective journal or personal notebook, and this can take many forms: it could be a bound notebook, a ring binder full of papers, a computer memory stick or an audio tape. Indeed, the whole idea of 'journaling' has itself become a focus for research and commentary. The work of Moon (1999b) is of considerable influence, with Cowan and Westwood (2006) also providing some interesting views on the subject. They discuss the results of asking experienced university teachers, who already required reflective journal writing from their students, to make the same demand of themselves with their own professional development in mind. Such interest has led to universities and colleges making advice on journaling available to their students – for example, the University of Worcester (2006).

It is not surprising that 'journaling' has its origins in diary writing and the work of philosophers who used the process as a means of enhancing creativity and professional practice. Perhaps a useful description of the 'journal' comes from Smith (1999, 2006). He suggests that a journal is a 'friend that is always there and is always a comfort'. He says that 'In bad moments I write, and usually end up feeling better. It reflects back to me things that I can learn about my world and myself.' Another view comes from Cooper and Stevens (2006), who suggest that journals can be used to create conversations about work and life, to organize work experience, to adapt journal-keeping practices to match current needs, and to review and reflect on career goals. They see journaling as part of lifelong learning and perhaps this tells us that journaling should not be seen in itself as a means of 'doing reflection'. It is just another strand in the make-up of professional and reflective practice. Its value is all the more apparent when it is seen alongside other facets of good practice. For example, allowing a focus on assimilating the views of others, sharing good practice and exchanging views, especially about differing values and beliefs. When this is allowed to happen it can lead to another strategy, which is encouraging communication between participants and asking that they co-construct solutions to problems, evaluate process and celebrate success. It prompts them to ask 'why', 'what', 'how' and 'who' questions.

Of course, we should not ignore the role of those who 'deliver' professional development; this would include tutors having a shared view of the values and beliefs that underpin the programme. Where this also includes a system of mentorship, it is argued that this brings significant benefits to those taking part (John 2006; Robbins 2006). Access to a mentor allows participants to consult with someone who shares their experience of the workplace, and facilitates an exploration of participants' work practices and needs. This is intended to build confidence, assist with goal-planning and help the integration of theory with practice. Mentorship is a formal role recognized with time and space for the participants to consult with their mentors. Within other forms of continuing professional development, the demands of time and finance inhibit such a formal arrangement, and support may come from a critical friend or workplace colleague.

Therefore, there are structural, logistic, personal and social strategies that can be employed in order to facilitate reflection as part of professional development. There is also a need to focus upon 'good practice'. One view is that this can be accomplished by participants following an established series of workforce competencies or outcomes – for example, those indicating the practice requirements of practitioners and leaders of children's centres (DfES 2007a 2007b). This will again promote a debate about how a set of technical requirements can represent good practice. However, engaging in such a debate may itself be part of the reflective process. To this should be added a clear understanding of what reflective practice involves and, where necessary, it should challenge assumptions about the nature of reflection, rather than assume that every person will immediately become a convert to the process. Overall, professional development should form a framework that provides a gradual and progressive focus upon key issues that are important to the participant and have a direct impact upon their practice.

## Conclusion

It is hoped that this chapter may prompt you as an early years practitioner to consider your own personal development plans. You may even be moved to picture what your professional life may be like in the future. Will the proposed changes in structure and organization of early years care and education affect day-to-day practice and policy at local level? How will you respond to change? Will change become an accepted part of your professional life? What might be the longer-term impact of such change on your own career development? Will this include engaging in professional development specific to obtaining promotion and leading a children's centre? These may be just a few of the questions you may ask yourself. Perhaps you may also be prompted to make a considered judgement about the notion of reflective practice, and ask if you feel confident about exploring your own practice values and beliefs. If the answer is yes, you may consider finding out if 'reflective thinking and practice' are indeed integral parts of any continuing professional development available to you – in essence, to help you on the journey that takes you towards being a competent, adaptive and reflective practitioner.

## References

Bolton, G. (2005) *Reflective Practice Writing and Professional Development* (2nd edn). London: Sage.

Brownlee, J. and Bethelsen, D. (2006) Personal epistemology and relational pedagogy in early childhood teacher education programs, *Early Years*, 26(1), March: 17–29.

Buchanan, M., Morgan, M., Cooney, M. and Gerharter, M. (2006) The University of Wyoming Early Childhood Summer Institute: a model for professional development that leads to changes in practice, National Association of Early Childhood Teacher Educators, *Journal of Early Childhood Teacher Education*, 27: 161–169.

Clegg, S., Tan, J. and Saeide, S. (2002) Reflecting or acting? Reflective practice and continuing professional development in higher education, *Reflective Practice*, 3(1): 131–146.

Cooper, J. and Stevens, D. (2006) Journal keeping and academic work: four cases of higher education professionals, *Reflective Practice*, 7(3), August: 349–366.

Cowan, J. and Westwood, J. (2006) Collaborative and reflective professional development: a pilot, *Active Learning in Higher Education*, 7(1): 63–71.

Craft, A. (2001) *Professional Development: A Practical Guide for Teachers and Schools*. London: Routledge.

Department for Education and Skills (DfES) (2003) *Every Child Matters*. London: DfES.

Department for Education and Skills (DfES) (2004) *Five Year Strategy for Children and Learners*. London: HMSO.

Department of Education and Skills (DfES) (2005) *A Sure Start Children's Centre for Every Community, Phase 2 Planning Guidance (2006–08)*. London: DfES.

Department for Education and Skills (DfES) (2006) *Children's Workforce Strategy: Building an Integrated Qualifications Framework*. London: DfES.

Department for Education and Skills (DfES) (2007a) *Children's Workforce Strategy Update – Spring 2007: Building a World-Class Workforce for Children, Young People and Families*. London: DfES.

Department for Education and Skills (DfES) (2007b) *National Standards for Leaders of Sure Start Children's Centres*. London: DfES.

Department of Health (DoH)/Department for Education and Skills (DfES) (2004) *Executive Summary. The National Service Framework for Children, Young People and Maternity Services*. London: DoH/DfES.

Dewey, J. (1933) *How We Think: A Reinstatement of the Relation of Reflective Thinking to the Educative Process*. Chicago, IL: Henry Regner Publishers.

Fowler, K. and Robbins, A. (2006) Being reflective. Encouraging and teaching reflective practice, in A. Robins (ed.) *Mentoring in the Early Years*. London: Paul Chapman.

John, K. (2006) Encouraging the discouraged to encourage the discouraged to encourage the discouraged ... Supporting the leaders of the new integrated children's centres, in P. Paola and A. Millar, C. Shelley and K. John (eds) *Adlerian Society (UK) and the Institute for Individual Psychology Year Book. A Collection of Topical Essays, 2007*. Chippenham, Wilts: Anthony Rowe.

Labour Party (1997) *Labour Party Paper: Early Excellence A Head Start for Every Child*. London: The Labour Party.

Labour's Early Years Task Force (1994) *Statement of Intent*. Millbank, London: Labour Party.

Manning-Morton, J. (2006) The personal is professional: professionalism and the birth to threes practitioner, *Contemporary Issues in Early Childhood*, 7(1): 2006 42–51.

Moon, J. (1999a) *Reflection in Learning and Professional Development*. London: Kogan Page.

Moon, J. (1999b) *Learning Journals: A Handbook for Academics, Students and Professional Development*. London: Kogan Page.

Moon, J. (2004) *A Handbook of Reflective and Experiential Learning*. London: Routledge Falmer.

Morley, C. (2007) Engaging practitioners with critical reflection: issues and dilemmas, *Reflective Practice*, 8(1), February: 61–74.

Moss, P. (2006) Structures, understandings and discourses: possibilities for re-envisioning the early childhood worker, *Contemporary Issues in Early Childhood*, 7(1): 30–42.

NPQICL (2004) *National Professional Qualification in Integrated Centre Leadership*. NCSL Triumph Road, Nottingham: National College for School Leadership, Pen Green Leadership Centre, www.ncsl.org.uk/programmes/npqicl/index.cfm (accessed 18 February 2007).

Osgood, J. (2003) Deconstructing professionalism in early childhood education: resisting the regulatory gaze, *Studies in Continuing Education*, 25(2), November: 5–13.

Osgood, J. (2006) Contemporary issues in early childhood editorial. Rethinking 'professionalism' in the early years: perspectives from the United Kingdom, *Contemporary Issues in Early Childhood*, 7(1).

Pen Green Leadership Centre (2007) *The Development of Government Policy in Early Years Leading to the Establishment of Children's Centres*. Unpublished paper, NPQICL Programme.

Reflect Project (2007) www.reflect-project.net (accessed 12 March 2007).

Robbins, A. (ed.) (2006) *Mentoring in the Early Years*. London: Paul Chapman Publishing.

Schön, D. (1983) *The Reflective Practitioner: How Professionals Think in Action*. London: Temple Smith.

Smid, G. (2001) Consultants' learning within academia: five devices for the design of university-based learning opportunities for management consultants, *Studies in Continuing Education*, 23(1): 54–70.

Smith, M. (1999, 2006) Keeping a learning journal, *The Encyclopaedia of Informal Education*, www.infed.org/research/keeping_a_journal.htm (accessed 12 February 2007).

University of Worcester (2006) *Study Skills Advice Sheet – Journaling*, www2.worc.ac.uk/studyskills (accessed 11 February 2007).

Whalley, M. (2006) Children's centres: the new frontier for the welfare state and the education system? Engaging with the struggle. *Paper presented at the Early Interventions for Infants and Small Children in Families at Risk conference, Grand Hotel, Oslo, Norway 27–28 April 2006*, www.ncsl.org.uk/publications/publications-c.cfm (accessed 20 January 2007).

# 11 Reflection and developing a community of practice

## Alice Paige-Smith and Anna Craft

This chapter explores how early years professionals can be considered to be a community of practitioners sharing both experience and issues that they need to negotiate within their role. We explore ways in which early years professionals can carry out research as a way of reflecting on their practice, both within and across settings, in particular in relation to a leadership role.

## Reflections on experience

Clough and Corbett (2000) suggest that as practitioners working with young learners, we meld the personal with the professional, drawing on our personal histories. As they put it: 'Tracing origins helps us to understand something of where we find ourselves today' (Clough and Corbett 2000). They refer to the concept of the 'lived relationship', personal and professional 'journeys'. These consist of accounts that include personal and professional views and experiences, and illustrate that, as they put it, 'systematic thought, analysis and theorizing are quite continuous with and expressive of the wider life experience' (2000: 38). They argue that our professional identities and our 'distinctive and influential perspectives' (2000: 38) are determined by what we learn, both professionally and personally, over time.

Such learning is drawn on experience; practitioners therefore engage in 'linking analytical thinking to their own experience of practice' (2000: 38). As explored elsewhere in the book, this linking occurs in many ways: through evaluating or researching experience, through a range of means, including documenting the experiences of professionals, parents and children through observations, images, interviews, questionnaire surveys, a reflective diary, listening to children (Clark 2004), and policy analysis or analysis of documents. In becoming who we are as practitioners, then, we build on layer upon layer of experience – our own, and that of others, generated by working within various communities.

In the following extract, Mel Ainscow, Professor of Education, reflects on his role within inclusive education:

I am engaged in the development of practice. I work with schools. I work with teachers. I work with Local Education Authorities. I think that I am very good at working with people and I, therefore, make things happen or help to make things happen because of that skill. I see myself essentially as a teacher. All the best things I have done have involved me working with groups of people all the time, where we have developed some initiative to make something happen or overcome something. I seem to have a skill in helping people to think together, to overcome problems, to be energetic. (Ainscow 2000: 41)

Ainscow has conducted large-scale research projects, on a local, national and international level, and has written about 'effective schooling' and inclusive education. At the same time, he reflects on how he sees himself as a teacher, a practitioner in his role, which involves exploring and developing practice.

What he describes reflects a keen awareness of his relationship with others in his practice. For Pollard (2002), whose seven features of reflective practice were referred to in Chapter 1, dialogue with colleagues was a vital element. But rather than being just one of a relatively large number of features, perhaps for those working in the early years in the early twenty-first century, what Wenger calls the 'community of practice' is an encompassing frame/ assumption for reflective practice.

## Developing a community of practice

The notion of the community of practice, which is referred to in a number of places in this book, has been developed from work by Lave and Wenger (1991), focusing on the socially situated aspects of learning. It signifies the social learning processes that occur when people have a common interest or area of collaboration over an extended time period where they can problem-find, share ideas, seek solutions, build innovative practices. Wenger (1998) has taken the notion of community of practice much further than its initial usage, seeing it in terms of the interplay in negotiation of meaning, and the brokering of shared understanding of change. Effective change or development depends on shared understandings. He discusses a number of tensions. Of these, it is the tension between participation (involvement/shared flux) and reification (congealment of ideas) that has had the greatest influence in the workplace. These tendencies are, according to Wenger, in continual tension between one another; reification, the process of abstracting and congealing ideas (as, for example, represented in symbols and written documents), is necessary in providing structure and a common reference point for understanding. And yet, alone, it is insufficient:

the power of reification – its succinctness, its portability, its potential physical presence, its focusing effect – is also its danger ... Procedures can hide broader meanings in blind sequences of operations. And the knowledge of a formula can lead to the illusion that one fully understands the processes it describes. (Wenger 1998: 61)

At the other end of the spectrum, and in tension with reification, is participation, which demands active social engagement in brokering meaning. Wenger suggests that participation is necessary to temper both the ambiguity and the inflexibility of reification. And, as he notes, there are practical consequences of this belief, in offering participants in a community of inquiry both the authority and the resource to decision-make:

If we believe that people in organisations contribute to organisational goals by participating inventively in practices that can never be fully captured by institutionalised processes ... we will have to value the work of community building and make sure that participants have access to the resources necessary to learn what they need to learn in order to take actions and make decisions that fully engage their own knowledgeability. (Wenger 1998: 10)

For Wenger it is a dialectical relationship. Neither reification nor participation can be understood meaningfully in isolation from one another in relation to the building of a dynamic community of practice; this is because a community of practice is evolving, learning and not static. When reification and participation interact appropriately, Wenger refers to this as 'alignment' of individuals with the community's learning task, directing energies in a common cause; the challenge, particularly in a multi-disciplinary environment, is to link specific efforts to broader styles and approaches such that others can invest their own energies and interest in them:

With insufficient participation, our relations to broader enterprises tend to remain literal and procedural: our co-ordination tends to be based on compliance rather than participation in meaning ... With insufficient reification, co-ordination across time and space may depend too much on the partiality of specific participants, or it may simply be too vague, illusory or contentious to create alignment. (Wenger 1998: 187)

The notion of the community of practice has fired the imagination of professionals and workers in many different contexts. It is suggested (Hildreth and Kimble 2004) that this may reflect the capacity of the concept of community of practice to provide those working in rapidly and continuously changing environments that may have a strong sense of uncertainty within them, with a means to develop some sense of shared meaning, ownership and even control over what is valued and recognized as 'appropriate practice' in the relevant disciplinary area. Organizations are moving rapidly away from structure, routine, hierarchies and teams, towards much more fluid networks/ communities, which are reliant on shared knowledge. Communities of practice are seen as a fluid self-organizing structure that may facilitate such a shift in practices. In a globalized economy where knowledge is distributed over flexible networks often geographically dispersed, the community of practice has gained huge interest from business in offering a means for knowledge management. But it has also begun to influence and inform the work of many professionals, including those in the early years sector.

The community of practice, according to Wenger (1998), whose further work on the concept has been and continues to be influential in many contexts, is a collective endeavour and is understood and continuously renegotiated and rebrokered by its members. Membership of a community of practice emerges through shared practices; participants are linked through engagement in activities in common. It is such mutually focused engagement that creates the social entity of the community of practice. The community of practice, which is established on some kind of common ground, endeavour or interest, builds up, collectively, an agreed set of approaches, understandings, values and actual communal repertoire of resources over time. These may include written and other documentation, but also ethos, agreed procedures, policies, rituals and specific approaches. Wenger notes that a community of practice may often be intrinsically motivated – in other words, driven by its members – rather than an external force. Communities of practice share and write an ongoing narrative. They evolve; their function is to reflect collaboratively on shared issues and to develop a story and collaborative approach, together. They often depend heavily on the informal relationships between people and, as ways of working that are often informal, as the relationships develop, so do sources and approaches to legitimation, as well as experiences of trust and identity.

While communities of practice often form within single areas of endeavour or knowledge, they also provide a means for complicated, multidisciplinary teams to function together to achieve common goals. The concept of community of practice seems to have much to offer the development of practice in the early years, and in particular the notion of brokering across perspectives – or the idea of the 'boundary encounter', which helps each community to define its own particular identity and approach to practice. This depends on the exchange of perspectives from one community of practice to another, and its success depends on skilful 'boundary straddlers' who are able to facilitate reflection on and exchange of perspectives. As Wenger acknowledges, this role is a complicated one, however it facilitates a 'participative connection ... what brokers press into service to connect practices is their experience of multi-membership and the possibilities for negotiation inherent in participation' (Wenger 1998: 109). To an extent this means practitioners recognizing and surfacing their own boundary experiences. For example, many early years practitioners are also parents themselves, their dual roles as parent and professional in a setting may, at times, complement or contradict each other.

Professionals who work with young children in England are required to fulfil a range of policy-based expectations within their provision, relating to curriculum, assessment and access to learning opportunities. Policy frameworks offer a focus that brings colleagues and others (including parents) together as a 'community of practitioners', to develop shared approaches to how they provide for and enhance children's experiences in early years settings. This requires a commitment to shared reflection on practice over time. As Wenger (2005) notes:

> Sustained engagement in practice yields an ability to interpret and make use of the repertoire of that practice. We recognize the history of a practice in the artefacts, actions, and language of the community. We can make use of that history because we have been part of it and it is now part of us; we do this through a personal history of participation. As an identity, this translates into a personal set of events, references, memories, and experiences that create individual relations of negotiability with respect to the repertoire of a practice. (Wenger 2005: 152)

Wenger notes that when practitioners are in a community of practice they can handle themselves competently and can understand how to engage with others. Apart from being able to negotiate a way of working together through experiences within the workplace, practitioners also draw on shared experiences and, through reflecting together on these, evolve collaborative/ shared perspectives: 'We learn certain ways of engaging in action with other people ... It is a certain way of being part of a whole through mutual engagement' (Wenger 2005: 152).

## Reflection and inquiry in building communities of practice

Within any setting, whether early years or another context entirely, there will exist varied perspectives, rooted in each practitioner's sense of identity within that setting or context. Born of each person's interpretation of their role in the setting, practitioner identity manifests itself in the tendency to come up with 'certain interpretations, to engage in certain actions, to make certain choices, to value certain experiences – all by virtue of participating in certain enterprises' (Wenger 2005: 153). Developing a community of practice involves the explicit reflection on practice, and sharing of and debate around differences, as well as commonalities.

Reflecting on practice can be carried out through certain types of inquiry/research-based activities and, as Aubrey *et al.* (2002) note, the prevalence of 'action research' within the early years field which includes data collection and change in practice. They also outline the ways in which ethnography presents an appropriate methodology for collecting data with young children. The data can include video- and audio-taped recordings; 'thick description' or contextual data; observations of individual participants, field notes, diaries, and other such documentary evidence from the research setting and the wider context. Both of these methods (action research and ethnography) can be carried out by 'insiders' in the research context, and being a practitioner carrying out action research or ethnographic research can enhance the collection of data. Aubrey suggests that ethnography 'makes explicit to a community, that which they already know implicitly' (Aubrey *et al.* 2002: 138) and the process of finding out about this allows observed communities to understand themselves in more depth. At the same time she suggests there is a lack of a general theory of education or learning in early childhood, and that questions which should be considered, might include 'How do young children learn?' and 'What role do adults play in that learning?'

## Collaborative and collective leadership

Essentially reflecting on practice, then, particularly with others, can be seen as an active process of collective meaning-making and assumes that every person is in a position of leadership in the development of a community of practice. For reflection takes every person into a leadership space to an extent.

Reflection may involve taking a 'balcony perspective', where you step back and see the bigger picture, complicated by several factors, including other people's hidden agendas, as Heifetz and Linsky point out:

> Fortunately, you can learn to be both an observer and a participant at the same time. When you are sitting in a meeting, practice by watching what is happening while it is happening – even as you are part of what is happening. Observe the relationships and see how other people's attention to one another can vary; supporting, thwarting, or listening. (Heifetz and Linsky 2002: 75)

Becoming an observer, they suggest, can also involve sitting back when making a point, pushing the chair a few inches away from the table, resisting the urge to sit forward, ready to defend the point you have made.

Empathy for others and expertise are also considered to be important qualities of leaders – however, as Maccoby (2000) argues, many leaders are narcissists, listening only for the kind of information they seek and behaving over-sensitively to criticism. Leaders may hold the following qualities, according to Goleman (1998: 41):

- a passion for the work itself
- seeking out creative challenges, love to learn and take great pride in a job well done
- an unflagging energy to do things better
- persistent with questions about why things are done one way rather than another
- eager to explore new approaches to their work.

These qualities may be observable among some practitioners in leadership roles – and identifying these, and some of the previous qualities highlighted (such as empathy) may constitute the role of the early years professional in a number of different settings. Empathy for the children is of course essential when working or simply 'being' with young children. Alice Miller (1995), in her book *The Drama of Being a Child*, writes about one situation:

> A family with a boy about two years old was asking for an ice cream. Both parents were licking their ice-cream bars on sticks and offering the boy a lick of their ice cream and telling him that a whole ice cream was too cold for him. The boy refused his father's offer of a lick of his ice-cream, crying out 'No, no' and tried to distract himself, and gazed up enviously at the parents eating their ice cream bars. The more the child cried, the more it amused his parents who were telling him that he was making a big fuss and it wasn't that important. The child then began throwing little stones over his shoulder in his mother's direction, but then he suddenly got up and looked around anxiously, making sure his parents were still there. Once the father had finished his ice-cream he offered the stick to the child and the little boy licked the wood expecting it to taste nice, he threw it away and a 'deep sob of loneliness and disappointment shook his small body'. (Miller 1995: 81)

Alice Miller observes how the child had no advocate, was unable to express his wishes and was opposed by two adults and their 'consistency in upbringing'. As she notes:

> Why, indeed, did these parents behave with so little empathy? Why didn't one of them think of eating a little quicker, or even of throwing away half

of the ice cream and giving the child the stick with a bit of ice-cream left on it? Why did they both stand there laughing, eating so slowly and showing so little concern about the child's obvious distress? (Miller 95: 82)

Miller suggests that these judgements and types of behaviour by adults are influenced by the adults' own childhood experiences. Being aware of the adult's role and the child's feelings involves empathizing with the child, while at the same time being aware of one's adult values.

Being an early years practitioner, then, in a community of practice, whether a solo nanny or childminder, a nursery worker or a teaching assistant, involves the planning of activities that nurture the child's learning, as well as develop a sense of well-being, *and* reflecting on one's own goals for the children, one's own perspectives for specific activities or provision. This may involve complex decision-making based on how children are participating in the setting alongside others, together with an awareness and knowledge of relevant curriculum policy documents. We *also* engage as reflective practitioners at the additional level of connection with other adults, within an evolving community of practice. And, as the early years setting becomes increasingly multi-professional, the development of such communities seems not simply useful but necessary.

## Points for reflection

- How do you 'work together' with other practitioners, parents or even the children? How do you share your practice within your context? (For example, do you share policy documents, is there a school council for the children to represent their views, how do you listen to parents, children and other professionals?)
- What is your own experience of working with another professional in your field who you consider to be a good 'leader' of practitioners or of practice?
- How do you consider this person to provide an example of leadership that you would like to follow? Can you provide examples of their practice that you would absorb into your own practice?
- What experiences do you have of Wenger's notion of 'boundary work', brokering understandings across different perspectives or roles (for example, sharing perspectives with health professionals responsible for the same children)? What facilitates and inhibits such encounters in your experience?
- How can the concept of a 'community of practitioners' help early years practitioners to reflect on and enhance practice?

# References

Ainscow, M. (2000) Journeys in inclusive education; profiles and reflections, in P. Clough and J. Corbett (eds) *Theories of Inclusive Education*. London: Paul Chapman.

Aubrey, C., David, T., Godfrey, R. and Thompson, L. (2002) *Early Childhood Educational Research: Issues in Methodology and Ethics*. London: Routledge Falmer.

Clark, A. (2004) The Mosaic approach and research with young children, in Lewis, V., Kellett, M., Robinson, C., Fraser, S. and Ding, S. (eds) *The Reality of Research with Children and Young People*. London: Sage.

Clough, P. and Corbett, J. (2000) *Theories of Inclusive Education*. London: Paul Chapman.

Goleman, D. (1998) What makes a leader, in *Leadership Insights* (*Harvard Business Review* Article Collection). Harvard: Harvard Business School Publishing Corporation.

Heifetz, R. and Linsky, M. (2002) A survival guide for leaders, *Leadership Insights* (*Harvard Business Review* Article Collection). Harvard: Harvard Business School Publishing Corporation.

Hildreth, P. and Kimble, C. (eds) (2004) *Knowledge Networks: Innovation Through Communities of Practice*. Hershey, PA: IGI Publishing.

Lave, J. and Wenger, E. (1991) *Situated Learning: Legitimate Peripheral Participation*. Cambridge: Cambridge University Press.

Maccoby, M. (2000) Narcissistic leaders, *Leadership Insights* (*Harvard Business Review* Article Collection). Harvard: Harvard Business School Publishing Corporation.

Miller, A. (1995) *The Drama of Being a Child*. London: Virago.

Pollard, A. with Collins, J., Simco, N., Swaffield, S., Warin, J. and Warwick, P. (2002) *Reflective Teaching: Effective and Evidence-Informed Professional Practice*. London: Continuum.

Wenger, E. (1998) *Communities of Practice: Learning, Meaning and Identity*. Cambridge, UK, and New York: Cambridge University Press.

Wenger, E. (2005) *Communities of Practice – Learning, Meaning, and Identity*. New York: Cambridge University Press.

# Postscript: Democratic reflective practice in the early years

## Alice Paige-Smith, Anna Craft and Michael Craft

### Conceptions of childhood guiding reflective practice

At the heart of the development of reflective practice and inter-professional collaboration, are shared and conflicting perspectives on how we see childhood itself in contemporary society. Society has moved far from considering the child as a blank slate, 'only as white paper, or wax, to be moulded as one pleases' (Locke 1693), or imbued with innate innocence or purity (Rousseau 1762).

In many parts of the world we now support a strongly child-centred and organic approach following the work of, for example, Benjamin Spock and Penelope Leach, after the Second World War, and reaching a new perspective with the notion of safeguarding children's rights (UN Convention 1989) and ensuring their social, health and economic well-being (DfES 2003). We now work within a range of complementary legislation to ensure equality in terms of ethnicity, disability and gender – all of which, set in historical context, is relatively recently developed – and all of which applies, of course, to Early Years.

### Reflective practice in the policy context

In Chapter 1 we quoted Yelland and Kilderry (2005) in posing the question that must be asked by all those working in Early Years and all those caring for under-5s, whether they be professional workers or not:

> In what ways can we create effective learning environments?

This book has sought to bring some coherence to the many possible answers to this question within a rapidly connecting context in both national and local policy, in which health, education and welfare workers are now close collaborators in the service of nurturing the child.

In addition to the national policy context highlighted in many of the preceding chapters, which have explored the implications for reflective practice of policies – such as *Every Child Matters* (DfES 2003), *The Ten Year Childcare Strategy* (DfES 2004), *The Childcare Bill* (HMSO 2005) and the introduction of Children's Centres (DfES 2005) – the work of early years practitioners is also impacted by extensive research in neurobiology. Key findings in studies from this area in the late twentieth and early twenty-first centuries have highlighted the importance of positive early experience (Huttenlocher and Dabholkar 1997; Kaufman and Charney 1999; Siegal and Hartzell 2003) and the social consequences of poor or insecure attachment (Lieberman and Zeanah 1995). Such research underpins many Early Years initiatives stemming from policy frameworks. One of the authors of this postscript was involved, in the early 2000s, in a Trailblazer Sure Start programme, in a deprived part of a large urban conurbation, where best results flowed from research, robust user satisfaction surveys and the observations of staff, which found that projects such as 'Here We Grow' (Visionpoint Report 2004; Asmussen 2004) built on the broad literature on attachment and the social reality of children's lives. The process of learning was reflective for both staff and users (see Figure P.1).

For staff, the reflections showed that critical elements in this programme were found to include:

- parents, carers and children working together in structured and extended creative play and learning based upon documented parental needs and living circumstances
- overt respect for and use of ethnic and cultural differences
- the availability of affordable childcare
- the inclusion of fathers.

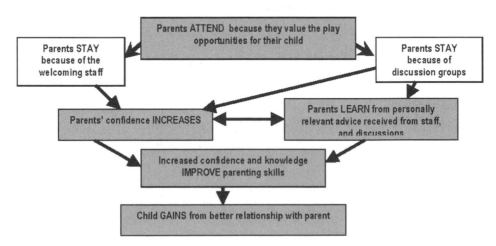

**Figure P.1:** Here we grow: the reflective process of learning
*Source:* Asmussen (2004)

Such initiatives and other, perhaps less radical ones, occur in a rapidly shifting context of policy and practice where inter-professional practices and the blended provision of integrated services are rapidly being introduced for young children. The following five principles were used as points of reflection by a group of Sure Start local programmes in London:

1. Parenting – the critical issue of good early attachment
2. Prevention – early action to avoid problems
3. Partnerships – working with all other key agencies
4. Participation – involving families
5. Planning – using evidence of good practice to plan ahead

These principles indicate the importance of teamwork alongside a community focus with other professionals, parents and 'the family'. A consideration of what is considered to be good practice and sound evidence for planning can be developed through reflection on practice. Each of the chapters in this book expresses an exploration of evidence of practice that supports children's learning and development.

## Multiple identities: towards democratic reflective practice

How can early years professionals maintain their own professional development through reflection in such a rapidly shifting environment? The authors who have contributed to this book have explored ways in which we may consider ourselves to be part of a community of reflective practitioners, in so far as there may be a shared sense of identity through working within settings that support and develop the learning of young children.

A key element in the development of inter-professional communities of practice in the early years is leadership of the team by senior reflective practitioners. In the first years of the twenty-first century, explorations were made by policy-makers (DfES 2007) and commentators (Moss 2003, 2007b) around the potential offered by the notion of the pedagogue, a highly educated childcare worker with leadership responsibilities. Peter Moss describes the role of the pedagogue as centred around a holistic notion of 'the child':

> The pedagogue sets out to address the whole child, the child with body, mind, emotions, creativity, history and social identity. This is not the child only of emotions, the psycho-therapeutical approach, nor only of the body, the medical approach, nor only of the mind, the traditional teaching approach. (Moss 2007b)

The function of such a senior and holistic role engaged in leading practice in early years settings has been emphasized in policy announcements, leading to the expectation that there will, ultimately, be an Early Years Professional role, which could be equivalent to a pedagogue, in every full daycare setting by 2015 (DfES 2007: 33). There appear to be expectations that those undertaking this professional role will take on leadership and/or management responsibilities, as well as being able to reflect on their practice and ensure that there are appropriate environments in which young children may learn and develop.

The expectation of the role of the Early Years Professional includes multi-agency working as well as building and motivating teams, and a capacity to understand multiple perspectives and identities. Both Linda Pound and Caroline Jones have, in this volume, considered aspects of leadership and team working within professional practice in the current context for the Early Years Practitioner. Ensuring the child is at the centre of early years practice has been considered through a 'listening to children' approach, as discussed by Elizabeth Wood in Chapter 7, and Alice Paige-Smith, Jonathan Rix and Anna Craft in Chapter 9. Michael Reed, in Chapter 10, considered how the early years practitioner can change and develop her/his own professional practice, perhaps leading to a questioning of what type of environment and curriculum should be created for the young child to learn. This central pedagogical issue has been discussed in Anna Craft's chapter (Chapter 6), focusing on creativity, and Jonathan Rix's chapter (Chapter 5), on inclusion.

A wider understanding of what it means to be a reflective practitioner has been a central focus of this book through the consideration of how to support and develop reflective practice, offering a model of *democratic* reflective practice. Drawing on the experiences of parents, professionals, practitioners and researchers in the early years, the book has sought to create a shared understanding of values, practices and approaches that support young children's learning, and proposes an understanding of the Early Years Practitioner as encompassing both the familial and the professional; a 'democratized' view of reflective practice, echoing views of the parent as competent and empowered citizen, and offering additional and valued views in dialogue with others, as proposed by Cagliari *et al.* (2004). Engagement with others within a community can be seen as building what Moss (2007a) refers to as democratic practice.

This holistic notion of reflective practice complements the conception of the child and of childhood as highly valued, nurtured and competent. A further dimension of reflective practice advanced by authors in this book is the contribution made by children's voices and perspectives on decision-making, reflecting the arguments by Clark (2004) that pedagogic documentation can be seen as a key tool for democratic practice.

## Challenges posed by democratic reflective practice

Tensions and dilemmas posed by an extended view of reflective practice are varied. They range from issues of pragmatics, to those that arise from contrasting paradigms or principles. Among the *pragmatic* issues is the vital question of how cultural practices are borrowed from and built upon as health, education and welfare are brought together more closely through policy. Take, for example, what can be learned from health about influencing behaviour. Evidence from the USA suggests that uncommon but embedded *positive* health behaviours in a given community (a 'naturally occurring' phenomenon) can be identified and disseminated to great effect in a process labelled 'Positive Deviance' (Marsh *et al.* 2004). Reflexive thinking was required to be open to this hidden resource: how do practitioners ensure that knowledge developed and understood within one community of practice, democratically informs others that overlap with it in the evolving early years practice?

There is a fertile policy/practice consensus at a national level in the UK and elsewhere focused on child health and well-being. For example, in Figure P.2 it is clear that the outcomes for *Every Child Matters*, objectives for Sure Start, as well as Standards for the Children's National Service Framework (DoH 2004), overlap comfortably.

| *Every Child Matters* outcomes ⇨ | BE HEALTHY | STAY SAFE | ENJOY AND ACHIEVE | MAKE A POSITIVE CONTRIBUTION | ACHIEVE ECONOMIC WELL-BEING |
|---|---|---|---|---|---|
| **Sure Start objectives** ⇨ | Improve children's health | Improve children's health | Improve learning | Strengthen families and communities | Improve availability, accessibility, affordability and quality of childcare |
| | | Strengthen families and communities | Improve social and emotional development | | Strengthen families and communities |
| **Children's National Service Framework Standards** ⇨ | Promoting health and well-being | Supporting parents or carers | Growing up | Family-centred services | Family-centred services |
| | Children who are ill or in hospital or disabled | Safeguarding welfare | | Complex needs | Mental and psychological well-being |
| | | | | | Maternity |

**Figure P.2:** The policy and practice consensus on child health and well-being

The challenge to the practitioner team is to develop a shared understanding of all three – and other – frameworks in fostering holistic practice with children, where views and perspectives are of equal value and worth, and multi-agency perspectives, where these exist, are valued.

Equally challenging in terms of pragmatics may be the hierarchical structures implied by the introduction of Early Years Practitioner Status and the notion of the pedagogue in settings that formerly had no one in this raised-status role, offering the opportunity for engaging in new ways with many others.

Many other practical tensions may be experienced by practitioners developing inter-professional working. These include evolving an understanding of the perceptions and perspectives of colleagues in related professions; also developing ways of sharing knowledge and learning together to support children and their families effectively.

Among the issues that arise from contrasting paradigms or principles are potential tensions inherent in the development of professional standards for those involved as professionals in contrast to the informal nature of parent engagement, with the differing degrees of compulsion and expectation attendant for each role.

There may also be fundamental tensions in developing a community of reflective practice where democratic principles underpin activity, at the same time as operating a setting as a business and offering a service in the marketplace. As Moss puts it, practitioners operating a business 'cannot allow democratic practice to be first practice because their primary responsibility is to their owners or shareholders; business decisions cannot be made democratically' (Moss 2007a: 18).

We would argue that our strength, in an inter-professional community of practice, is sound knowledge and the opportunity is sharing and negotiating this in partnership with colleagues and service users. We have identified some possible pragmatics and principles that may inhibit this vital growth in democratic reflective practice. But are there other weaknesses or threats? Those in leadership roles must be aware of the hidden weakness of tightly controlled and narrow professional practice, and the threat of fluctuating national policy with its drive for targeted outcomes within what may sometimes feel to practitioners like unrealistic timeframes. For all in early years, reflecting in or on professional practice in a democratic way means recognizing and hearing varied perspectives on such barriers, through professional processes such as self-assessment, line management, appraisal and training, much of which involves sensitive and aware leadership.

Other than these challenges, some of which arise from ambitious and far-horizon-focused policy-making, the sky is the limit for those of us working with young children. Let us take full advantage of the current opportunities, and as we do so remember that thoughtful documentation will provide vital evidence for our development of democratic, collegial reflective practice.

# References

Asmussen, K. (2004) The evaluation of 'Here We Grow', *Sure Start Evaluation Report*, National Evaluation of Sure Start website: http://www.ness.bbk.a-c.uk/documents/findings/1157.pdf (accessed 14 June 2007).

Cagliari, P., Barozzi, A. and Giudici, C. (2004) Thoughts, theories and experiences for an educational project with participation, *Children in Europe*, 6: 28–30.

Clark, A. (2004) The Mosaic approach and research with young children, in Lewis, V., Kellett, M., Robinson, C., Fraser, S. and Ding, S. (eds) *The Reality of Research with Children and Young People*. London: Sage.

Department of Education and Science (DES) (2007) *Children's Workforce Strategy Update*. London: DES.

Department for Education and Skills (DfES) (2003) *Every Child Matters*. Nottingham: DfES.

Department for Education and Skills (DfES) (2004) *Ten Year Childcare Strategy*. Nottingham: DfES.

Department for Education and Skills (DfES) (2005) *Children's Centres*, http://www.everychildmatters.gov.uk/earlyyears/surestart/centres/ (accessed 11 May 2007).

Department of Health (DoH) (2004) *Children's National Service Framework*, http://www.dh.gov.uk/en/Policyandguidance/Healthandsocialcareto-pics/ChildrenServices/Childrenservicesinformation/index.htm (accessed 13 May 2007).

HMSO (2005) *The Childcare Bill*. London: House of Commons.

Huttenlocher, P.R. and Dabholkar, A.S. (1997) Regional differences in synaptogenesis in the human cerebral cortex, *Journal of Comparative Neurology*, 387: 167–178.

Kaufman, J. and Charney, D.S. (1999) Neurobiological correlates of child abuse, *Biological Psychiatry*, 45: 1235–1236.

Lieberman, A.F. and Zeanah, H. (1995) Disorders of attachment in Infancy, *Infant Psychology*, 4: 571–587.

Locke, J. (1693) *Some Thoughts Concerning Education*. London (reprinted by Hackett in 1996).

Marsh, D.R., Schroeder, D.G., Dearden, K.A., Sternin, J. and Sternin, M. (2004) The power of positive deviance, *British Medical Journal*, 329: 1177–1179.

Moss, P. (2003) *Beyond Caring? The Case for Reforming the Childcare and Early Years Workforce*. London: Daycare Trust.

Moss, P. (2007a) Bringing politics into the nursery: early childhood education as a democratic practice, *European Early Childhood Education Research Journal*, 15(1): 5–20.

Moss, P. (2007b) Presentation at the Society for Educational Studies Annual Meeting, November.

Rousseau, J.-J. (1762) *Émile*, available in edition translated and annotated by Allan Bloom (1991). London: Penguin.

Siegal, D.J. and Hartzell, M. (2003) *Parenting from the Inside Out*. New York: Penguin.

United Nations Convention on the Rights of the Child (1989), Children's Rights Network, http://www.crin.org/docs/resources/treaties/uncrc.htm (accessed 12 June 2005).

Visionpoint (2004) Sure Start Evaluation Research. Job no SS315, in http://www.haringey.gov.uk/scrutiny_review_of_sure_start.pdf: 32–47 (accessed 14 June 2007).

Yelland, N. and Kilderry, A. (2005) Against the tide: new ways in early childhood education, in N. Yelland (ed.). *Critical Issues in Early Childhood Education*. Maidenhead and New York: Open University Press/McGraw-Hill Education.

# Index